DRAGONS ——

THE MODERN INFESTATION

Dragons are powerful, mysterious, wise and beautiful beyond
the beauty of any other living creatures. They ennoble the
human spirit. They are Man's fittest companions, save God.

Juan Tomás San Miguel de los Robles

The discipline of verminology calls for rigorous ordering of
an elegant, beguiling, and often overwhelming complexity.

*Philip Marsden, to the first graduates
of the New Zealand School of Dragon Studies.*

I. Titus. This photograph was taken by Philip Marsden as angry dragons emerged from their cave on the first night of the Disaster. The light areas of the plate show the typical incandescence of an aroused worm. The bright spots are sparks, possibly dust motes ignited by the heat of the dragon.

(*Photo: Science Museum/Science & Society Picture Library*)

DRAGONS —

THE MODERN INFESTATION

Pamela Wharton Blanpied

THE BOYDELL PRESS

First published 1980

Reissued 1996
The Boydell Press, Woodbridge
Reprinted 1997

The Boydell Press is an imprint of Boydell & Brewer Ltd
PO Box 9, Woodbridge, Suffolk IP12 3DF, UK
and of Boydell & Brewer Inc.
PO Box 41026, Rochester, NY 14604-4126, USA

ISBN 0-7394-0158-0

Contents

I   A SHORT HISTORY OF THE MODERN INFESTATION AND THE DEVELOPMENT OF VERMINOLOGY

II   ANATOMICAL AND BEHAVIORAL CHARACTERISTICS

III EXCERPTS FROM THE PAPERS OF MARTA FROEDLICH AND PHILIP MARSDEN

List of Illustrations

Abbreviations

ABD	*Anatomy and Behavior of Dragons*
ADC	Air Defense Command: North Atlantic Treaty Organization
AnatLat	*Anatomista Latinoamericano*
BolEsBA	*Boletin de Estudios Cientificos*
CSN	*Canadian Science Newsletter*
CompAnat	*Comparative Anatomy*
CompBlgy	*American Journal of Comparative Biology*
DNDI:OP	*Dragon, Non-Dragon Interface: Occasional Papers*
DNDI:SIP	*Dragon, Non-Dragon Interface: Studies in Ingestive Preference*
DNDI:TDD	*Dragon, Non-Dragon Interface: Techniques of Deterrent and Defense*
DSG	United States-Canadian Dragon Survey Group
DSGDP	*DSG Dragonographic Publications*
ICA	International Congress of Anatomists
LY	*Long Yanjiu, Beijing (Peking)*
Lex	*Lexicon of the Percussive Language of Dragons*
NADC	North American Defense Community
NFR	*Nagata Foundation Review*
NR	Nagata Reports
NZJV	*New Zealand Journal of Verminology*
NZSDS	New Zealand School of Dragon Studies
NZSDSWP	*New Zealand School of Dragon Studies Working Papers*
RCMP	Royal Canadian Mounted Police
RevChi	*Revista Chilena de los ciencias naturales y sociológicas*
RevZoo	*Revista Zoológica*
USAF	United States Air Force
USADC	United States Air Defense Command
USDOD	United States Department of Defense
ZR	*Zoology Review*
ZooJ	*Zoological Journal*

Preface to 1996 Edition

This new edition of *Dragons: The Modern Infestation* is presented by his many friends in the verminological community in honor of Sean Jones, Distinguished Professor of Verminology and Director of the New Zealand School of Dragon Studies, upon the occasion of his retirement. It is reissued as it appeared thirty-five years ago, five years after Professor Jones had left his verminography professorship at the University of Toronto to join Philip Marsden here in New Zealand.

As Director, Professor Jones has guided the School through a very difficult transition. His patience and his vision have not, perhaps, prevailed as he could have wished. His tenure has spanned a period from sparse to plentiful dragon populations. With the world now embroiled in an explosion of dragons, the focus of verminology has perforce shifted from language and communication to a more realistic arena. Though our efforts must now be concentrated on defense, we honor Professor Jones, here, and congratulate him on his work.

The year Professor Jones assumed the Merino Chair at NZSDS he also presided over a meeting of the International Association of Verminologists in Christchurch. The keynote speech was delivered by his mentor and colleague Philomel St James, then Professor of Verminology, Emeritus. That speech is reproduced in this commemorative reissue to recognize and celebrate the scholarly rigor and creative enthusiasm Professor Jones has brought to the study of dragons.

Frances Granita Bedford, Chair
International Association of Verminologists

II. Scarborough Head, New Zealand. The sheer cliffs are a popular launching area for
Knotting and are reputed to be the starting point for flights to the
west coast of Chile. (*Photo: L. MacDonald*)

Address to the
Seventh Biennial Congress
of Verminology

Philomel St. James

You, gathered here, are being very kind to an old woman. This is the Seventh Biennial Congress of Verminology and it will be my last, as you know. I look out across this room full of friendly and familiar faces and I am profoundly grateful to have had the opportunity to work with you and watch you assume your places in the vanguard of the rising generation. You are hopeful; you are often wise; you are full of purpose. The world rounds to your vision of how things are and how they should be. And though you wish me well and more than well, honoring me as no one deserves, and you have waited without impatience as I made my way up the last stairs to this podium and the end of my public career, you are ready to move past me and into what comes next. That is as it should be.

It is time for verminology to move on, beyond me and all that I represent as the last living person who sat at a plank table under an open sky and broke bread with Philip Marsden and Marta Froedlich and that charming and funny walnut of a man, Baodelio Santander. Your link with them will now be Sean Jones and you are, if I may say so, a lucky bunch to have him. Treat him well; he has the beast at his back.

This is taking on the elegiac tone I have always distrusted. Eighty-seven is not so old as all that. Forgive me. What I want to tell you, since you have invited me to speak, is what my experience with dragons leads me to believe is on the horizon.

First, know that I know that this is all speculation. Even in human affairs speculation is only tenuously useful; with dragons it is laughable.

Next, know that I concede that I was born in the early decades of this Infestation and I am hopelessly outdated.

Third, know that I am convinced that I am right. I'm old enough to respect that and to know – at the same time – that it doesn't make a piffle of difference whether I'm right or not.

That out of the way, let us think together for a few minutes about the beasts that bring us together in this wonderful hall with the wide windows opening to the Pacific. The dragons seem to have been very quiet lately. I think it has been fifteen years since we have had any sort of major outbreak. Even in the Faeroe Islands dragon Chant has hardly been heard above the waves. Sean Jones nods to agree, I see.

When he was young, in his early thirties, he floated, prone, on a balsa wood raft in the Sargasso Sea with dragons all around him basking in the sun, eyeing him, ignoring him, waving their tails and the tips of their wings at each other, content. The murmuring blurble of their conversation could have lulled him to sleep, had he been unwary. For years now such a raft would have floated mile after mile with only seaweed for company. Dragons have not been eating sheep from New Zealand's high pastures like corn off a cob. They have not festooned themselves across the overpasses of major highways or draped their sinuous lengths around skyscrapers. Their attention has been elsewhere. They have been ignoring us and that has lulled us into thinking we understand them.

Thirty years ago when Philip retired as head of NZSDS, dragons were everywhere. Intercontinental air traffic patterns shifted daily to avoid them. Their stench flowed across the grazing lands of every continent. There were Verminologist Reports on the nightly news with colorful world maps detailing the day's sightings. The Boumani Sonic Net screeched and flashed like the Fourth of July in New York Harbor.

One afternoon, before this building was built, I sat on that promontory over there and sketched young dragons playing on the beach forty feet below. They were fishing, or learning to fish, in that sportive, violent way they have. They were young, less than a year old certainly. Ten of them, two families, maybe three month's difference in ages between the two roils. The quarry was seals. This was a seal colony at that time. There were maybe a hundred seals with pups crowded onto the rocks. An acre of seal meat conveniently crammed into a small cove, it was easy prey for the dragon kits. The bull seals bellowed and flopped, but the cows and pups and the bulls themselves were gone in less than an hour. When that game was over, the kits flew off banging and clanking, on to another game. One of the adults stayed long enough to finish off the last of the wounded seals left rolling and helpless in the blood-stained breakers.

We live now with only the rumor of dragons. Have even ten of the verminologists in this room seen a dragon cross-stitching, black, against a clouded sky? Half of you are working on materials derived from materials deduced from papers written on manual-keyed computers.

I look down the schedule for this conference and see that the major issue to be considered is classification. A lot of heat is generated over this issue. Shall dragons properly be termed 'bi-alar-quadrupeds'? Where do they fit in the taxonomy? *Chiroptera*? Ridiculous. They aren't bats. *Reptilia*? I see Torontonians smiling. The five toes, the horny-plated armor – and yes, the young are shell-born miniature adults and do not suckle, not mammal babies at all. But what do we say to six, jointed, appendages? Shall our dragons, then, be grouped with the larval-younged *Arthropoda*? Not a good fit. Besides, six legs *and* a back bone? (The representatives from the European universities are smiling now). In the absence of any physical remains, aren't we, all of us, deducing the insides of dragons from their appearance? Isn't this a kind of reverse of the way we deduce the appearance of dinosaurs from the stony evidence of their bony insides? Are dragons oxygen-dependent *Animalia* at all? Now the graduate students are carefully not smiling, but gentlemen and ladies, does it matter?

Another half day of this conference is devoted to the comparative analysis of percussive Chants. Now this is my own field, but a half day? In these papers you are sifting dust. There are no new recordings here. You all know the annotation system, but not three people in this room can understand those sounds when they hear them. Departments are torn apart over questions of whether the percussive 'flaah' should be written with an umlaut.

Here is what I think: we don't have the time.

Funding is drying up. Dragons are being downsized from Beijing to Johannesburg. Even in Houston and Khartoum, capitals of the feeding stations of the world, there is no interest in dragons. In Argentina they are circulating a petition to repeal the Official Toleration Act so they can expand pampas grazing areas beyond the safeguards. They are even building homes in Invercargill, perching them on the hills to capture views of Stewart Island. Dragons are being, once again, slowly but surely, relegated to children and the crackpot verminologists like you and me. We are being crowded onto a narrow beach, and we are fighting each other for shrinking squares of pebbly ground.

Meanwhile – and here I know I will sound like Cassandra – beasts who have spent decades in quiet Observation are rousing, rising from the ocean floor, drifting down from the Andes and the rocky caves of the Himalayas, having a look around, getting a little peckish. And we know from Zoology 101 what happens next: feeding, hoarding and, most ominous of all, mating.

It will start out small, I think. More sightings in populated areas. A few head of cattle here and there. People will dig out articles from forty years ago. There will be documentary histories. New theories will be formed as the beasts start to intrude further and further into human affairs.

This renewed interest will mean money. You will be suddenly very much in demand. Funds and fame will flow into your departments again. The corset of scientific rigor will slowly unlace. Papers will be written with titles like 'Sapient Partners: Interspecific Communication for the Twenty-Second Century' – 'Verminological Solutions to Resource Recovery: Implications for the Paramushir Peninsula' – 'The Dragon as Tool in the Reclamation of Agricultural Land' – 'The Eighth Intelligence: The Role of Dragon Speech in Early Childhood Education'. The military will gladly, generously and secretly help you explore ingenious new weapons designed to penetrate what you will tell them are vulnerable spots in dragon anatomy.

Publicly, dragons will be wildly popular. There will be dragon film festivals and dragon chat groups, dragon healers and dragon corporate consultants to revolutionize the bottom line. Politicians dressed in jungle fatigues and flak jackets will look for a treaty-signing claw to shake for the cameras. Apparatus will be designed to fit onto the backs of dragons so that humans can ride them, or ride with them, into outer space or to the bottom of the sea. Enormous effort will go into finding a beast to elucidate the physical history of the earth and the meaning of life. Bogus books of 'as told to' dragon memoirs will convince even sensible people that dragons are helpful half-angels keen to lend a hand. Women's groups, men's groups, whole families will backpack into the bush seeking salvation by kindly dragon.

There are no kindly dragons. *Chordata* or *Arthropoda*, umlaut or not, that dragon pair boiling the waters of Sydney Harbor in a Knotting dance so expressive of all that is majestic in the universe, so potently beautiful that you will forget to breathe through your open mouth – that is a pair of dragons: supremely powerful, implacably un-human, and, most relevantly of all, fertile.

But I could be wrong. This Infestation could be over entirely, not poised for the next breeding cycle and the interspecific chaos that implies. You will figure it out. I will leave you to it with my blessing and my hopes. And with this:

Those of us who have shaped our ears and minds to hear *Dragon* don't talk about it much these days. *Dragon* is out of fashion. It requires such an effort to translate into the speech of everyday life, and it is based on such radically odd assumptions, there aren't that many occasions. But, being attuned to them, we do see dragons, daily when we are lucky. I haven't talked in public about it much but I think maybe it is time.

As you know, I have spent the last eighteen months on the road. I am, I guess, a kind of talisman, a witness to the interpenetration of human and dragon life. People don't know what to do with me, really. Many, maybe most, doubt that dragons exist and suspect that I'm crazy, but they want to be able to say they have heard me play a Chant. And my job, as I say, is to bear witness.

What I want to tell you is that I have seen more dragons this trip than I could list in an all-day session of this Conference. Many more on this trip than the one four years ago.

Most of you know that when I traveled with Philip Marsden from Ascension to Marta and Baodelio's hidden house on the coast of Brazil, I met two beasts who have been more or less constants in the sixty-or-so years since. 'Rosa' and 'Jim', Marta called them, kits from a roil she knew on the Taitao Peninsula of Chile during the first breeding cycle of this Infestation. These two no-longer kits have looked me up from time to time, keeping tabs on an old acquaintance, appearing suddenly and vividly just to say hello. Some of the repairs on the roof of the building where my office is are due to the stresses of their rather clumsy landings. When the School was new and Philip was still around, they used to hang over the edge and peer in the windows of that building, looking for us. I saw Jim yesterday, floating quietly on the breeze, half in mime, checking out the cattle in Heathcote Valley. I saw Rosa last week on that ridge that runs along the San Andreas Fault on the Peninsula south of San Francisco.

But there are dragons everywhere now, not just Jim and Rosa. A big blue-gray one I had never seen was clinging to the bottom of the Bay Bridge, thrumming with the traffic, letting the wheels roll over his toes, dangling his head down to the water to watch the boats. No one seemed to notice. When I was speaking in North Carolina two weeks ago the countryside there was visited by four or maybe five dragons who otherwise perch on hilltops outside Asheville. From the corner of my eye I saw one lift a heifer out of a field and fly off with it to a quiet place to chew. Mateo, a roil mate of Jim and Rosa, alternates Observation around Durham with lolling idly about in the Atlantic between Cape Hatteras and

Ocracoke where he can fish without spending an ounce of effort. I haven't seen Mateo in twenty years. Why is he suddenly on the scene?

In other words, my dear friends and colleagues, wake up. You are thinking too small. Read your papers to each other if you must, but get up. Get out of this hall. Stand in the wind on Scarborough Head and look around you. Listen. Hear what is there to hear. Dragons.

Introduction

Dragons are finally accepted as part of the natural order by most people. But although we have all felt some of the more drastic effects of their active presence in the world – the Disaster and the Worm Levy, for instance – there is a general ignorance about the beasts themselves: their habits, anatomy, psychology, and life cycles. This is caused partly by the failure of the popular media to deal with any but the most sensational aspects of dragons as they impinge upon human activities. Few people have any direct contact with dragons, so we are dependent upon the reports of others for most of our information. Of course it may be that a general knowledge is enough. From media reports we know that dragons are dangerous and that they can be very destructive. That is all we really need to know about cyclones, after all, and the man who has lost his family, his home, and his livelihood to a twister is not likely to need meteorological details. He and his neighbors will be sufficiently wary. But dragons are more than merely destructive, and even more than destructive and fabulously wealthy. So the scientific study of dragons, though at a very primitive stage, yields information about the beasts that can be rewarding to anyone with a sense of wonder and a curiosity about the natural world.

The wages of ignorance are illustrated in an account of one of the earliest encounters in the United States. On the afternoon of June 23, 1967, a dragon was spotted on the dairy farm of Earl J. Fulton, near Marengo, Iowa, west of Cedar Rapids. This dragon was feeding – taking two cows with their calves in the space of three hours. Mr Fulton saw no way to intervene between the dragon and the terrified stock, and the cattle would not respond to his efforts to herd them to safety. Thoroughly frightened, he locked himself and his family in the house and spent a restless night wondering if he had been hallucinating. In the morning he ventured out to retrieve his herd and found that the dragon had disappeared after eating the choice cuts from four cows and two calves. We now know that this dragon was probably satiated at that point and would have been content to observe the rural scene for a few days before returning to a more remote area. However, Mr Fulton was enraged by the loss of his stock and fearful for the safety of his farm and his family. He called the local police, who made a routine visit to humor him. Dragons had never been sighted in that area, and confirmed sightings in other locations were not widely reported. The police assumed that Mr Fulton was either mentally deficient or the victim of a hoax.

However, even a casual glance at the field confirmed that something had happened, as there was evidence of scorching and trampling, and the cattle and hogs could not be herded. The police could find no trace of a dragon, although his scorched trail led quite clearly to the southeast through two ponds that had been drained, ending in a cluster of small hills. The search continued until nightfall. Early the following morning one of the Fulton children saw the dragon in the air flying toward the farm. The police responded to the call and notified the state troopers. A SWAT team organized a thorough search and at noon located the dragon sleeping in a ten-acre woodlot on a neighboring farm. The worm was aroused by the search party and flew off, leaving their ears ringing with a derisive bellow.

He reappeared two days later on a bluff overlooking the Cedar River. He became absorbed in Observation. When several days of inactivity passed, an enterprising travel agent from Cedar Rapids organized tours to view the beast. Four buses made the trip in safety. The tourists became bolder as the worm did not respond to being photographed or shouted at through bullhorns. However, on the second day of tours the first busload carried equipment designed to stir him up a bit: cattle prods and fireworks. The dragon killed the entire busload. He deposited the driver's body some distance away from his observation site in dense bushes and proceeded to eat the fleshy parts of all the passengers but two old men.

At this point the dragon was labeled a menace and the National Guard was called in. Long-range ballistics were employed – mortar and artillery – but the dragon proved to be too difficult as a target. US Army films of this portion of the incident show the dragon moving from a mood of stubborn enjoyment of the river view, to vague annoyance, to a delight in playing hide-and-seek. Reinforcements arrived, bringing bazookas and flamethrowers. The bazookas were useless, but the dragon was surprised and amused by the flamethrowers, stamping his feet with pleasure. Rearing to his full height, spreading his wings to present the largest target, he taunted the Guard, flying over their heads and shooting flames in imitation of their weapons. Anti-aircraft fire proved ineffective against so skillful a flier. A guerrilla-trained team bellied through the grass under low bushes to attempt a close-range attack with machine-gun fire. The dragon camouflaged himself and they crawled past him. At four-thirty the Guard regrouped to plot strategy. The dragon dozed and finally flew off in a leisurely way shortly before sunset, leaving the people of Cedar Rapids to bury their dead, sadder and no wiser.

The purpose of this monograph is in part to forestall that kind of destructive encounter between the species by making available to the general public the research on dragons that has been completed since the first modern sightings about one hundred years ago, in the hope of fostering a better understanding of the risks inherent in dragon-human contact, and a deeper appreciation for the beauty and the complexity of these beasts. The recent death of Philip Marsden, the premier verminologist, has prompted this effort to correlate the information in the field for the first time for a general audience.

For the newcomer to dragon studies this should serve as an introductory text, however brief. It includes a short account of the beginning of the Modern Infestation and the growth of the science of dragon study. Part II is a crude description of the beast himself: his anatomy and the metabolism that makes him unique, his habits, and his life cycle. These form the heart of dragon studies. The foundations of the science of verminology were laid by the Brazilian anatomist

III. Philip Marsden. (*Photo: George B. Wharton, Jr*)

Marta Froedlich and her outstanding pupil, Philip Marsden. Without these two investigators there would be no science of dragons. The third section consists of a selection from the personal papers of Froedlich and Marsden. These are included even though they are informal in nature and may lead to misinterpretation, because they give a 'feel' for dragons that the reader otherwise could get only from personal contact with the beast himself.

There is an ongoing debate in the verminological community concerning the inclusion in the literature of the field of nonquantitative material like the firsthand accounts of Part III. The proponents of value-free analysis do not insist that all nonquantitative material be excluded, but only that some objectively verifiable standards be met. The community at large concurs and complies with these informal guarantees of scientific reliability. The chief resistance comes from the faculty of the New Zealand School of Dragon Studies itself. Their insistence on the validity of strictly nonquantifiable information is, as they themselves freely admit, largely the result of their tradition of requiring students to acquire a basic familiarity with dragon language. The verminological community asserts that unless specific data from field reports can be confirmed by second and third experiments in the field, the data cannot be accepted as more than informal opinion.

For example, the New Zealand School of Dragon Studies has assumed that dragons are equipped with all higher cerebral functions. But until intelligence quotient assessment indicators can be devised and proved to be accurate, this is a nonverifiable assumption, and conclusions based on this assumption cannot automatically be accepted as valid. Verminologists who converse with dragons are emotionally involved with their subjects. They come to believe, apparently, that their enthusiasm for these creatures has to have been caused by intellectual parity between the species. Thus, though verminologists trained at the NZSDS are often superb observers, they cannot be expected to draw objective conclusions from the data they have collected so carefully, often at great personal risk.

The material included in Part II, 'Froedlich's Experience with the Roils of Taitao', was excerpted by the publishers and distributed to the media before publication of this book in spite of the vigorous opposition of this author. It became popular overnight, has been translated into thirty-two languages, and is now familiar worldwide. Perhaps the success of this portion of the book will promote readership and further the cause for which the book was written. If so, it will partly repair the damage caused by premature publication of this sensational material without background information or critical comment. Ms Froedlich herself and Philip Marsden were careful to publish only the quantitative aspects of their work. The next generation at the New Zealand School of Dragon Studies might do well to follow the example of the founder of that institution and confine themselves to the limits of value-free analysis. The professional verminologist leaves aside nonquantifiable data, folk accounts, and other popular sources of information, and relies solely on substantiated evidence from the scientific community, except where instances from subjective accounts and from archaic traditions can be seen to reflect accurate information gathered from at least one legitimate source. Dragon Chants may be lovely to hear and elaborately constructed; the Knots may be beautiful and complexly executed; the beasts apparently do speak, but we cannot upon this evidence draw the conclusion that dragons are in fact as intelligent as human beings. Bird songs, spider webs, and parrots urge us to caution. The reader should keep this in mind when he is confronting the Froedlich experience in the roil, or an analysis of dragon language, and while he is reading Part III of this work.

For those interested in further reading, publications from the University of Khartoum are recommended, as are random articles in the Proceedings of the Fifty-eighth and Fifty-ninth International Congress of Anatomists, and the publications of Froedlich and Marsden. Stephen Lucan's *The Destruction of San Cristóbal* is an interesting description of a plundering dragon. *The New Zealand Journal of Verminology* and the *New Zealand School of Dragon Studies Working Papers* should be studied with the bias of that school in mind. Bruford's account of the pursuit of the 'Dragon Book of All Time' can be read with profit if the reader is prepared to make distinctions between fanciful and actual sightings. Material from earlier times is of historical interest, of course, and may be informative if proper cultural allowances are made. Those interested in the dragon lore from the Pre-Medieval Infestation may use any of a number of collections.

A note on terminology: many old names have been retained for convenient and perhaps romantic reasons. 'Dragon' itself is a hopelessly inadequate term, freighted with superstitious associations from three thousand years, but it is too well established to discard. The word 'mime' is not an accurate description of the dragon's extraordinary ability to assume the appearance of his surroundings, but it has entered the common parlance and so is used here. Similarly, the primitive 'fire chamber' for the digestive organs, and the coy 'roil' for a family of hatchlings have been retained since they are familiar, specific, and useful – though not particularly accurate. Liu's naming of sexually immature dragons 'stern' and 'stiera' for male and female is only marginally useful, since sex specificity is not important in dragon behavior or biology except during the infrequent mating periods. It should be noted that young dragons are called 'kits' until they reach the Wandering stage. No one who has watched a young kit tear the hindquarters off an ox without pausing in flight would be tempted to call him a 'dragonette'.

The author wishes to thank colleagues in the Dragon Study Group for their patient co-operation, and the dragonologists of the New Zealand School of Dragon Study for allowing examination of the unpublished papers of Philip Marsden. Particular thanks go to Ruth Kimmerer for her assistance with the Latin American materials, to Neil McMullin for his translations of the Hashima expedition field notes, and to Giovanni Pani, Bruce Bennett, James Carley, and E. Effron for sharing their editorial and critical skills. The personal papers of Froedlich and Marsden have been made available by the kindness of Philomel St. James and Sean Jones. Research for the preparation of the monograph was carried out with the generous support of the Witkin Foundation and the Brewster Oliphant Center for the Investigation of the Natural World, which also provided invaluable resource material.

Part I

A SHORT HISTORY OF
THE MODERN INFESTATION AND
THE DEVELOPMENT OF VERMINOLOGY

The Beginning of the Modern Infestation

Although most sources have dated the beginning of the Modern Infestation period at about the turn of the century, a fresh examination of the historical materials makes it clear that there was a dragon population in the world as early as one hundred years ago, and dragons may well have been significantly present before that.

Toward the end of the last century there was a series of mysterious 'fire falls' in western Canada, and scattered isolated falls throughout the North American continent, principally north of the 50th parallel, and in the same latitudes of the Eurasian continent. These falls remained unexplained and even largely unexamined, although similar phenomena were being reported out of Siberia and Argentina. For example, one mid-January toward the end of the last century a flaming object fell into the pond of a farmer in New Hampshire, disappearing below the ice. Radiation detection gear brought in by the sheriff's office showed extremely high levels of radioactivity, and the area was cordoned off by the National Guard. The day after the fall federal officers examined the pattern of ice cracks, drained the pond, and searched the mud. Their radiation gear showed a normal reading. The conclusion was that the local equipment had not functioned properly, and though something may have fallen through the ice, there was no evidence that anything unusual had happened. Complaints from dairymen in northern New Hampshire concerning the loss of cattle that week were not associated with the incident, nor were the forest fires in the Sherbrooke-Magog area of Quebec four days later, nor was the marked drop in deer population of the state that winter linked to the incident at the pond. Eventually this and similar falls were simply forgotten.

Official records show a gradual decline in beef supplies reaching Saskatoon and Edmonton during the last quarter of the century. Economically these were hard times on both sides of the border, and politically there were strains between the two countries that had not existed earlier. Ranchers in Montana, Idaho, and the Dakotas suffered unexplained losses from their herds, as did their counterparts in Saskatchewan and Alberta. Suspicion grew that there were rustling raids across the border and an organized foreign effort to sabotage the Canadian beef industry.

Plate IV. One of the earliest confirmed dragon sightings. This small West Virginia farm was haunted by curious, but phlegmatic, dragons for two years. At first puzzled and alarmed, the retired couple who owned the farm learned to accept their extravagant visitors as part of the natural environment, and there were no unpleasant incidents. (*Photo: NZSDS*)

Then came the great prairie fires and the destruction of the oil rigs in Alberta, which led to the tragic anti-US demonstrations in Calgary, Medicine Hat, and Regina. The series of Grand Forks-St. Boniface raids narrowly missed precipitating a complete break in US-Canadian relations. The heroic efforts of the people of Winnipeg to calm these hostilities have not received the commendation they deserved. In the cool light of history these events can be seen to be directly attributable to the beginning of the growth of dragon infestation and the ravages of the hungry, quarrelsome beasts.

The record of the early years of the Modern Infestation is a tribute to the human ability to insist that there is nothing new under the sun. Individual pieces of evidence, like the fall into the New Hampshire pond, or the prairie fires in Alberta, were fitted into explanations based purely on pre-dragon assumptions. If there is no culturally sanctioned explanation for an experience, we tend to ignore it or fail to notice it at all. In fact, without an interpretive system in place the experience cannot be experienced, and we will not know what is in our presence. To explain this process epigrammatically, if the concept '4' did not exist, '2 + 2' would always be only '2 + 2'. As Bronowski said, 'But, of course, as an idea [the electron] was inconceivable so long as it was believed that the atom is indivisible'. (Bronowski, *The Ascent of Man*, 330).

In the early years of dragon infestation, relationships between evidence were disguised and whole patterns overlooked simply because there was no culturally acceptable explanation that made their correct interpretation possible, no 'dragons'. There were not very many dragons at large on land, after all, and they did not linger undisguised in broad daylight close to human habitation. At the time of the Green Wilderness Report the total North American dragon population was probably not more than fifteen or twenty. World population on land was probably limited to between 150 and 170 active dragons. Eating only a half ton of food a week during normal feeding patterns, a dragon did not make heavy demands on the human population as a whole, though he might have been disruptive to his immediate neighbors. People who saw dragons in flight thought they were birds or aircraft: the distinctive shape of that particular bird was forgotten or ignored, there being no explanation to support the visual experience. Descending spouts of fire were labeled the re-entry of space debris, and groups like the Spotless Terrestrial and Astral Rights Society were formed to lobby for 'clean' space projects. The short-term, self-obliterating observation satellite was built in direct response to pressure from these groups. Significant numbers of cattle and other livestock slaughtered in the field were attributed to rustlers moving by helicopter, to inter-ranch warfare, or to meat growers protesting low prices by mutilating their own herds. In the USSR special guards were deployed to the largest beef-producing areas to prevent sabotage by dissident factions thought to be making a political statement in attacking the food supply. Private ships reported seeing unusual large creatures in the sea, but amateur sightings, even those by experienced amateurs like the fishermen of the *Hitachi Maru*, were easily dismissed as misidentifications of leopard shark or gar. Large, swimming, snake-like creatures in inland waters were explained as eunuch eels or, more adventurously, as prehistoric survivors. When repeated searches of legendary homes for these monsters revealed no hard evidence of their existence, the local stories were laid to the romantic imagination. The possibility that the 'monster' visited only periodically was not even considered. No blame should be placed on the preceding generation for not recognizing immediately that a creature known to them only in myths and fairy tales was in fact filleting the stock on the back forty.

Present ignorance, however, is more willful and less easily forgiven, once reasonable evidence has been presented. Many creatures live side by side with us and we are unaware of them. Every large Canadian city has a significant population of owls, raccoons, and opossums, though they are rarely seen. Coyotes roam New York City with impunity, but very few people are aware that their apartment trash cans are visited every night and that they themselves are carefully watched by pairs of yellow eyes if they venture into the streets after dark. But reports on these familiar creatures are greeted with surprise, not disbelief. No one doubts that there are whales in the oceans, though evidence comes second or third hand, and photographs of whales could be easily constructed in the darkroom. Yet the famous *Diario* photograph of the dragon 'Cortez' over the Zócalo in Mexico City was dismissed as a fraud by most of the responsible journalists of Europe, though they had no evidence to support their disbelief. Even people who have seen dragons accompanying plane flights or at a feeding site are not uniformly convinced that what they have observed is in fact dragon.

The most cogent argument against the existence of dragons is based on scepticism and economic realities. Since the Warley scandals many people are not inclined to believe the media without substantiating firsthand evidence. They argue that the media have been duped into reporting a ridiculous fabrication – dragons – as if dragons actually existed. They claim that the reports of dragon activity are part of an elaborate scheme to justify the Worm Levy. Dragons, they say, are the invention of a worldwide conspiracy foisted on a gullible public to facilitate the funding of unpopular federal and international programs without the introduction of any specific tax. Frederick Grundler's testimony before the United Nations Worm Levy Commission sought to substantiate this argument by reference to other tax subterfuges launched in the United States since the Taxpayers' Revolt. It is time that we set aside this kind of argument and came to terms with the fact that we are in the company of dragons.

Stewart Island and the Green Wilderness Report

The first officially recognized dragon sightings were on the South Island of New Zealand. But although photographs were published in the international press, the world at large either ignored or disbelieved the reports. The local population tolerated the dragons until they began to make serious problems for the sheep industry. After considerable debate the conservationist faction in the House of Representatives defeated the military-conservative proposition that the Governor-General be asked to petition the Crown to bomb and napalm the small dragon colony. Eventually the dragons were forced out by a canny policy of petty harassment: round-the-clock, blatant surveillance and exhaustive flash photography. The beasts retired to Stewart Island, where they descended in force at night without warning, destroying all human habitation, and established what has remained the most stable and jealously guarded dragon retreat. Subsequently under pressure from the dragons, much of the southern tip of the South Island was deserted and the city of Invercargill left virtually uninhabited.

Data from this period from South America below the 45th parallel are too sparse to draw any firm conclusions about dragon population there, though, using our present experience, we can reasonably assume that there were dragons scattered widely throughout most uninhabited areas, just as they were in the Northern Hemisphere at this time. There are no records from what was then South Africa, of course.

During this initial period of the Infestation, the caribou herds of the Northern Hemisphere shrank by more than 25 percent. Periodically in Canada and Alaska there were destructive fires that decimated other wildlife and destroyed many of the best natural habitats in that area, including salmon spawning ground. Environmentalists waged a bitter and sometimes violent fight against the oil and gas establishments of Canada and the United States, believing that the fires were a result of the leaks along the pipelines, and the loss of caribou the result of the disruption of the normal migratory patterns. The dramatic revelations of the Green Wilderness Society conservation group field study in the Northwest Territory convinced the North American public, as the Stewart Island disaster never had, that there was indeed a serious dragon problem. Here is an excerpt from that report (Green Wilderness Society: Northwest Rescue Committee Report No.1):

It is the conclusion of the Northwest Rescue Committee that the problems which instigated the formation of the Committee were caused in large part by a factor heretofore unknown in Canadian environmental studies: dragons. The Committee, therefore, recommends that the Green Wilderness Society modify its opposition to the petroleum industry, especially with regard to the pipelines and storage facilities in the Northwest Territory and Prairie regions. The pipeline and tanks that are already in place should be allowed to continue operation after sufficient safety measures are installed. Although the Committee has found that had these facilities not been in place during the last seven years, at least 92 percent of the total number of significantly destructive fires reported in the region would not have been introduced into the vulnerable habitat, the system of storage and transportation for petroleum-related products is sufficiently important to the prosperity of the Canadian people that the system should continue to operate without harassment by the GWS until the solar industry has grown sufficiently to make further use only marginally useful for the energy needs of Canada. However, these facilities must be guarded constantly against:

1. attack by saboteurs, especially by foreign nationals;
2. inadvertent attack by wild animals, as in the unfortunate rupture on the Calgary spur caused when a dragon stampeded six hundred and fifty head of beef cattle into the pylons supporting the line;
3. defects in the integrity of the line caused by inadequate safety

supervision and insufficient managerial inspection during the manu-
facture and installation of equipment.

The Green Wilderness Society should not hold the petroleum industry
responsible for the disruption in the natural balance in the environment
in the Northwest Territory, except insofar as fires spread by the introduction of petroleum products have destroyed existing populations or habitat.
The Committee recommends that the GWS not bring suit against the
industry unless it refuses to install sufficient remedial measures. The cattle
industry may indeed have cause to file.

The chief factor in the reduction of the populations of large herbivores and
predators, and the resulting imbalance in the environment, is beyond question
the introduction of a new predator at the top of the food chain: the dragon.

The Northwest Rescue Committee recommends that the GWS can be
most beneficially employed for the preservation of the Northwest Territory and the Prairies in three ways:

1. by co-operating fully with the petroleum and beef industries, the
    Canadian and New Zealand governments, and the military estab-
    lishment in designing and implementing a system of detection and
    defense against the dragon as predator. If the delicate balance is to
    be maintained in the wild areas, and if the cattle industry is to prosper,
    the responsible parties must be equipped to defend themselves, their
    livestock, and their wild cousins against predation by dragons, at
    least to the point where the existence of the industry or the wild
    species is no longer in question;
2. by assisting in the insertion of a foolproof system for averting the
    spread of fires caused by inadvertent dragon sparks, due to the
    introduction of petroleum products into locally insignificant burns;
3. by protecting petroleum industry installations from inadvertent dis-
    ruption by dragons, earthquakes, or by other natural disasters.

Military Response to Dragon Raids

After the Green Wilderness Society report and after the tragedy on New Zealand's
Stewart Island, the conservationist approach to dragon control was discredited.
There followed some twenty years of variations on the military response.

Dragons came under the jurisdiction of the defense establishments of the major
nations, including Canada. Marta Froedlich began her lifelong study of dragons
during the early part of this period, but she was unable to publish her work, and
the scientific study of dragon populations went unread. As time went on, she was
able to interest a few graduate students in her speciality, though the major portions
of her work still concerned reptilian biology. Aside from her small enclave at São
Paulo, no serious verminological studies were undertaken outside the military
during this time.

The first attempt at a census was made by the defense establishment, which reasoned that if the number of dragons and their principal meeting places were known, a more efficient defense could be devised. However, the technique for locating the worms in satellite photographs had not been developed, and land survey proved impossible. There was then, as now, the problem of accounting for dragons on the sea floor. The final count from this census is therefore very low, well below what were undoubtedly the actual numbers. The second census taken just thirty years ago took full advantage of satellite photographs and projected a possible figure for the ocean population by extrapolating from a series of samples taken with sonar readings in the South Atlantic and in the Pacific west of Cape Horn. The figures from this census should also be regarded as inaccurate. The satellite readings and the ocean samplings were taken over a period of many months, and a mobile dragon could have been counted three or more times. At present there is no evidence to justify the assumption that the population in the oceans is uniformly distributed. We will return to the census question later.

The military community was, and remains, unable to predict either the time or the location of dragon visitations. The beasts appear at will. An elaborate dragon-detection screen erected in the midwestern portion of the North American continent was in operation for twelve years. Although it did plot the flight of several dragons during that time, only two landed in areas prepared to deal with the beasts – one in Texas and one in Kansas. In both these cases, the deployment of ground defenses proved futile as the dragons came and went quickly, taking the prey they could get easily. A historical map of dragon raids in the North American continent over the past fifty years shows that they avoid heavily populated areas, and areas where pollution is heavy. Thus there are few raids on the eastern Seaboard and none in southern California. The spectacular raid on the St. Louis stockyard is clearly an anomaly. If the historical map is augmented with unexplained phenomena, like the New Hampshire incident described above, the pattern is enhanced. The destructiveness and frequency of the raids seem to ebb and flow, peaking every twenty-three years.

Even if dragon raids were predictable, the problem of defense would remain. Conventional military methods are not, as a rule, effective. Heat radiation from the beast produces a distortion similar to the refraction of water, but inconstant, so that accurate aim is not practicable, even if the beasts remain stationary. Added to this difficulty are their speed and maneuverability in the air, coupled with their shape – long but very narrow and flexible at every point, so that the target can change shapes radically every few seconds (USDOD:AF 736:491:4). They have the ability to camouflage themselves in the mime. In addition, they are intelligent, cunning, and, occasionally, playful.

The Disaster

The search for a weapon or series of weapons for dragon defense was pursued most energetically in Western Europe and the United States through the co-operation of the North Atlantic Treaty Organization. The culmination of these efforts came when a young dragon was wounded with a specially adapted heat-seeking missile as he flew over Hamburg. In the days that followed, Northern, Central, and Eastern Europe were visited with an unprecedented campaign of revenge by the wounded dragon and his companions. The notorious campaign, known as the Disaster, left the countryside between Groningen and Warsaw in ruins, with scattered incidents of destruction as far spread as Lyons, Salzburg, and Chernovtsy in the Ukraine. Contrary to the popular versions of the Disaster in the media, the dragons did not attack indiscriminately.

Nor did they single out young women and children for their victims as the recent broadcast, 'Lust of the Rapine Worms', so graphically and inaccurately portrayed. They descended on farms, large and small, and systematically burned all standing crops. News accounts contemporary to the actual event made a point of assuring their audience that no lives were lost to dragons (viz. *Die Welt,* or *Le Figaro*). However, since it was mid-August, dragon raids destroyed four-fifths of the agricultural production of the region and necessitated the slaughter of most of the surviving livestock, including poultry.

Europe spent a long, bitter winter importing virtually all its food supplies at enormous cost. This precipitated a serious international quarrel in which the Germans were blamed for their attack on the dragon, though all European and North American countries were armed similarly, and there had been official congratulations to the Germans from all neighboring countries for the success of their missile before the implications of their success became clear. Poland, East Germany, Denmark, France, and the Netherlands demanded reparations for the Disaster from the West German government, which did not have sufficient funds, even if it had accepted responsibility for the raids. Eventually the United Nations negotiated with the Middle Eastern-Mexican alliance for long-term loans, which enabled the European agricultural industry to be rebuilt. In the long run, of course, the Disaster has meant progress as well as ruin, since land-use patterns were obliterated by the fires and a more efficient farm technology is now practiced in Europe than had been possible previously. Whether or not this increase in productivity has been worth the cost remains a moot question. In any case, as a result of the Disaster, military response to dragon threats has been discarded, and we have settled for a variety of passive defenses based largely on sonic shielding and on our ability to predict likely targets and get out of the way.

Dragon Studies: The First Phase

When the military response was discredited, dragon studies began in earnest. Projects exploring speed and maneuverability, and statistical projections of sightings, were set aside. National and international funding became available, centers for systematic research were established, and long-range projects on dragon behavior were undertaken. Although she had been pursuing her interest in dragons in the time left over from her conventional work, Marta Froedlich was now free to begin the research for which she became famous. There were objections from her colleagues and the lay sponsors of her projects. They argued that dragons were too unreliable to be studied at close hand, too dangerous to be studied by women, too elusive to be studied in their lairs. Fortunately she was able to face down these arguments with the data she had been collecting in Chile with funding from the Latin American Coffee Growers Association. Her field techniques have remained the staples of dragon research: scientists with vigorous academic backgrounds in very small groups or alone, unarmed, supplied with only tape recorders, cameras, notebooks, and endless patience, prepared to spend long years in remote places.

At this time the University of Santiago published a study by Hernando del Fuentes and Carmino Garcia-Gil showing that though the incidence of dragon raids was uniform in the Northern and Southern hemispheres, when the figures were adjusted for population density (which would affect the recording of dragon sightings) and for desert conditions, the frequency of destruction and the actual losses were about double in the Northern Hemisphere (RevChi 143). This was true even when the raids of revenge were left out of the calculations. China, they noted, reported destructive raids at a level well below that of any other nation of either hemisphere. The del Fuentes–Garcia-Gil interpretation of these data followed the old Sino-Communist line: that dragons despised capitalism, colonialism, and socialist revisionism. The traditionalist Chinese on Taiwan seized on this obscure document and published sensational charges that the People's Republic of China was converting the natural resources of the Chinese homeland and the cultural heritage of all Chinese people into enormous bribes to any dragon venturing across Asian skies. These charges were ignored by the Mainland and greeted with scorn by the international community, who saw them as another example of the traditional bitter hostility. Froedlich was intrigued, however, and encouraged two of her graduate students to re-examine the Santiago paper.

Using the same data, but introducing a sliding formula to account for available plunder, they discovered that in the Southern Hemisphere destructive raids beyond a level they labeled 'tolerable' increased in frequency in areas that were urban or progressive, and decreased in areas where the population was rural, underdeveloped, uneducated, or stubbornly traditional. With funding from the Brazilian government these two students, Baodelio Santander and Emilio Branco, undertook field studies in three areas of low incidence of dragon destruction: on the Argentinian Plateau, in interior Brazil, and in Paraguay. They found a pattern of response to dragon sightings that was uniform for all three areas. (Subsequently this pattern has proved uniform throughout all low-destruction regions). When a dragon was seen in a rural area, the local people conferred, selected a spot midway between the village and the dragon, away from habitation, and left there a collection of valuables, jewelry, livestock, and, occasionally, a scapegoat from the populace, amounting to an offering. Sometimes the offering was ignored and the dragon disappeared; sometimes only the edibles were taken, or the best pieces of jewelry; sometimes everything was taken and the village and surroundings were devastated anyway. But the pattern clearly showed that dragon appetites could often be appeased with suitably rich tribute. The local people were in agreement that the dragon was likely to be a better bet than the government. In the Pampas the local expression was 'Como dragón regatea, no como policía' ('He bargains like a dragon, not like the police'), indicating a stiff price but an acceptable risk (Branco and Santander, BolEsBA).

After the publication of the Santander-Branco paper, the Canadian news media pursued the story in China and revealed that the Chinese government did in fact have an established policy of offerings to dragons, based on the old Chinese assumption that the dragon is a beast of good omen. When dragons were sighted for the first time, near Wuwei in Gansu Province, they were greeted with delight as a sign that good times were at hand. Subsequently one-tenth of each farm was cultivated for dragon use, and a tithe was collected on imports for the support of special currency minted exclusively for dragon offering. These coins were already being made at the time dragons were meeting in significant numbers on the South Island of New Zealand. The coins are intricately wrought, stamped with the characters for good fortune and gratitude, and made with the traditional hole in the middle so they could be strung on cords for the presentation ceremonies. They are made principally of gold and weigh twenty grams. This revelation shocked the Western nations at the time, though the Worm Levy is now commonplace in the West. However, the Western nations have not been able to welcome dragon visitations enthusiastically, and have never matched the success of the Chinese or the rural populations of the Third World in preventing destruction on a large scale.

The Hoard of the Worm of Nagata

Curiously enough, during the first fifty years of the Modern Infestation, the question of dragon hoards was ignored. For many years, of course, the beasts themselves were ignored and the hard evidence of their presence was explained by the manipulation of pre-Infestation phenomena. But even after the Stewart Island episode and the Green Wilderness Society report, when the beasts were accepted as regrettably real by the general populace, the question of hoards did not enter public discussion. Dragons were a military problem, and attention was focused on how to avoid contact with them. After the Disaster, when there could no longer be any doubt about the existence of the worms, when dragons and dragon studies became the legitimate property of the scientific community, the emphasis settled on behavior and reproductive studies. Rumors of dragon raids for plunder were discounted, though the Chinese and Santander-Branco reports gave them credence. Hoards were officially considered nonexistent, a wishful fabrication left over from the earlier infestation period. There were only scattered speculations on dragon gold in the popular press, principally references to the old stories.

Two years after the Disaster, a Japanese botanical expedition, headed by Hashima Masaharu, set out to collect samples from a neglected region in the Naga Hills on the India-Burma border in Assam. For centuries this sparsely populated area had been avoided by the local people, who regarded it as a haven for dragons, snakes, and demons. The Japanese team hoped to find botanical specimens untouched by modern pollution. When they arrived in Kohima and announced their intention of exploring the region for an extended period without taking any significant weaponry, the local people were alarmed and warned them excitedly that an enormous dragon had been sighted flying over the area for several weeks. They could not find local guides willing to go with them. The constabulary threatened to arrest them when they insisted on their intention. While they were in the constable's office, their hotel rooms were ransacked and their survival gear was stolen.

Outraged, they protested to the regional police and the federal authorities. They were placed under house arrest until word came from New Delhi via Gauhati, which would either expel them from the country or give them permission to continue their study. After six months they received an official communication: they would not be prevented from exploring the hills west of the Burmese border and removing legitimate specimens of genuine scientific interest, but they could not obtain local guides or help of any kind, nor could they expect any assistance from the national government on any phase of their project. They were permitted to navigate the Dayang River and were allowed resupply missions of not more than two helicopter flights a week. The official assumption was that the team would not survive a fortnight in the wilderness and the affair would be closed. The Japanese party set out the following day with supplies they had amassed during their long wait.

Fourteen days into the expedition, when they entered the highest elevations, they began to encounter areas of devastation. Quarter-acre sections were burned and trampled. They judged the marks to be at least three weeks old, since the vegetation had begun to regenerate. They did not speculate on the causes. On the afternoon of the eighteenth day they came into a small valley at the crest of a hill of about 2000 meters. All vegetation had been destroyed, and they calculated that nothing had grown there for decades. At the head of the valley in the face of a low cliff was an opening surrounded by debris. The whole area had been severely trampled and scorched. For the first time since they had entered India, they wondered if there might be something to the local superstitions. However, they had not seen even a large mammal during the entire trip, and dragons still seemed very remote indeed. They entered the cave to find it almost completely filled with an unimaginable treasure.

Fortunately the members of this expedition recognized the importance of their find and were not interested in plunder. They photographed the pile as it lay, beginning with the debris outside the entrance, recording every centimeter thoroughly. In the two months that followed, the Hoard was dismantled bit by bit, carefully described in a preliminary record, and packed into canvas bags. Helicopters arrived every three and one-half days, bringing in supplies of food, recording equipment, and empty bags, and leaving heavily laden. The treasure, disguised as field samples, was transported by two brothers of Hashima to Kyōto, where it was examined and catalogued by a skeleton crew of experts at the

University. The head of the University was introduced to the Hoard after the first three shipments made it clear that the project was going to have international significance and bring honor to the University and to Japan. All agreed with Hashima's team in the Naga Hills that any premature discussion of the find would mean disaster. The little group spoke privately with Kawasaki Yoshiaki, and he donated the funds for a lavish museum to house and display the Hoard. At his request and that of his family, the role they played in building this lovely museum has remained unknown, though the Kawasaki crest has been worked into a part of the border design at the right of the front entrance. The purpose of the building and the nature of the find remained secret until the work was completed two and one-half years later and the Hoard of the Worm of Nagata was unveiled to an astonished world. (Hashima and Taylor, *The Treasure of Nagata*).

Burma and India were incensed and demanded that the Hoard be delivered to them. The Japanese refused, citing the terms under which the expedition had been conducted. Indeed, the Hoard does not contain a preponderance of pieces from those two countries nor even from Asia. The Worm had ranged far afield, collecting from every continent and from the past seven centuries. With our current knowledge we can safely assume that he raided other hoards in amassing his pile, perhaps even gathering from hoards from the Pre-Medieval Infestation Period that had gone undetected in the peaceful interim. There is an abundance of pieces from the second and third centuries of the Common Era that could not have been readily available for plundering raids as we know them. Since there are no dragon-levy coins in the pile, though other Chinese artifacts are liberally present, it seems likely that this Worm was one of the first of the Modern Infestation to succumb to hoard lust. This helps to account for the richness and variety of the pile as well, though the aesthetic judgment of the individual dragon should not be discounted. It remains the most valuable hoard ever discovered, though the pile discovered in Siberia is also very rich and has its own intriguing collection of uncut gems and raw gold (NR23, 'Kirensk').

Hoard Fever

The opening of the Nagata Museum precipitated the first and most disastrous worldwide epidemic of hoard fever. The general public was, and for the most part still is, appallingly ignorant about the risks involved in any attempt to dislodge a hoarding dragon. There is no reliable record that any dragon has ever been driven off his hoard by any of the innumerable expeditions in this or the Pre-Medieval Infestation, though occasional hunters have survived. We simply do not have the technology to wrest control away from a hoarding dragon. Any weapon that would destroy the dragon would destroy the hoard. They find each other, of course, and a larger, more determined dragon can seize a pile guarded by a lesser worm.

Even if we could capture a hoard, the initial difficulty of locating it would remain. Not all dragons hoard, and those who do succumb to hoard lust do not do so in concert. There are probably no more than ten dragons in the world who are actively hoarding at any one time, and the hoards are secreted in inaccessible or uninhabited regions.

The hoards themselves are not uniformly valuable. Some are truly fabulous, as the Hoard of Nagata was, and that of Cortez undoubtedly is. Some, however, are quite puny, a few semiprecious stones and some costume jewelry or scrap metal representing perhaps a halfhearted collection, or a pile amassed by kits at play. Some are idiosyncratic. The pile at Tristan da Cunha was composed entirely of assorted mollusc shells. It was a beautiful collection of shells, and the University of Ābādān was delighted to receive it, but it did not meet the expectations or expenses of the expedition that had monitored the site in secret for fifteen years, waiting for the dragon to fly off. A hoard found at Revelstoke, British Columbia, consisted principally of gallon plastic jugs which a young dragon had apparently enjoyed melting under his curled heat. But the scarcity of plunder does not discourage plunderers, and no warning seems sufficient to cool hoard fever once it is ignited by the story of a sitting dragon or a deserted pile.

When the University of Kyōto opened the Nagata Museum to the public, literally thousands of people left their homes to pursue dragon gold, ill-equipped and completely ignorant of their prey. Wilderness areas from Hudson Bay to Cape Horn were ransacked. The rugged interior of the northern Eurasian continent was combed. The influx of hoard hunters caused a measurable improvement in the economies of Burma, Bangladesh, and India. There were deaths from snakebite, frostbite, tropical diseases, exposure, hypothermia, and from the foolishness of inexperience in the wild. There were deaths from the mishandling of equipment and weapons far too complex for amateurs; from intrigue, from murder, and from the desperation born of greed. Dragons were hunted scientifically with radio-interference and heat-detection equipment. They were sought by deductions from elaborate computer-plotted probabilities and by surveillance aircraft, and were run after pell-mell by anyone who had heard a rumor or thought he had seen a worm in the bushes. Scores perished in the flames or jaws of dragons who were not hoarding and who had actively avoided human contact for decades.

Legitimate projects of dragon research, so recently established, were thrown aside in the rush for plunder. Field teams engaged in the difficult task of locating and establishing trust with small dragon colonies were interrupted by hoard hunters and as often as not destroyed. Ornithologists, geologists, astronomers – anyone working quietly on a field expedition was endangered by hoard hunters. Eighty-five percent of the small bank of competent verminologists in the field were killed in the first onslaught of hoard fever, and their sponsoring institutions refused to continue their work.

Revenge, the Official Toleration Act, and the Consequences for Verminology

Dragon populations were quick to respond with characteristic ruthlessness to this outbreak of hoard hunting. Although their revenge was not on the scale of the Disaster, they made a clean sweep of all human habitation bordering their colonies. The remains of Invercargill, New Zealand, were completely obliterated in the space of one long night, though the canny New Zealanders had evacuated the remaining population at the first hint of trouble. Even in China, where dragons had been most amenable to bribes and persuasion, there was wanton slaughter in villages that had maintained relations of mutual tolerance for two or even three generations.

In the face of the destructive response by the dragon population, most of the major nations, north and south, outlawed hoard hunting within their borders and denied passports to those seeking to hunt abroad. After suffering especially violent reprisals, Chile, Argentina, and Korea closed their boundaries for two years to all tourist traffic whatsoever. Most countries made hoard hunting a crime on a par with murder, and strictly forbade human-dragon contact for any purpose.

By the end of the second year of the United Nations Official Toleration Act, hoard fever was under control. The incidence of unprovoked dragon attacks dropped. At the end of seven more years the situation worldwide had returned to its pre-fever state with one significant difference. Although dragons did not go out of their way to attack humans, they no longer tolerated them. They assumed, not without cause, that the man peering out of the bushes was a dangerous pest. All meetings of dragons with humans were fatal during the period. People learned to be terrified even by the sight of a dragon aloft. The experience of the last decades shows that actually a dragon in an area of human habitation is there for a short time: for food, for plunder, or for recreation. He is not there to attack the human population in ordinary circumstances. But the terror learned during the revenge period has not been unlearned in the ensuing years of quiet relations between the species.

The scientific and military investigation of dragons came to a standstill after the outbreak of hoard fever. Only Froedlich in seclusion in Brazil and Marsden isolated on Ascension Island were able to continue their work, in secrecy and by chance. Froedlich, now fifty-seven, went into semi-retirement, teaching one semester in four. She was regarded with suspicion and even contempt because of her familiarity with dragons, and only her distinguished work on the morphology of small reptiles prevented her dismissal from the University. Some friends allowed her to live in seclusion in a small house near Cananéia on the Atlantic Coast. The isolation from her regular duties allowed her to organize her field notes and begin the work on *La Morfologie de los Dragones*, and *A anatomia e comportamente dos dragões*. The police watched her house from time to time to prevent her from trying to conduct new field work with dragons. However, they had little control over the dragons themselves, and she received periodic visits from at least two young dragons who would spend a few days in the area and move on. The local people were terrified of the beasts. But since the dragons seemed content just to sit near the cottage, there was little the police could do to interfere.

Froedlich wrote the major portion of her early work on dragons at Cananéia, but she did not try to have it published, knowing that any attempt to circulate her work would give the government the excuse it needed to arrest her. Years later, after public opinion reverted to a more normal level, she began to publish in small journals circulated in the scientific community. Her true importance was not recognized until Marsden's notoriety in the media brought her publications to the attention of a larger audience and forced her colleagues to reassess her work in a new and largely unexplored field.

Marsden on Ascension Island

The other major figure in the field of dragon studies is Philip Marsden. Together with Froedlich, he established verminology as a legitimate field of inquiry. Without her interest he would never have begun dragon studies, and without his support her work probably would never have been recognized. Together they constructed a rigorous discipline and a systematic study out of a field ignored by the respectable scientists and infested by dreamers, quacks, romantics, and treasure hunters. Marsden's first important field work, which began three years before the Disaster, illustrates the methods of the serious verminologist and will serve as an example of the rigors of the basic research for this science. This famous study was conducted on Ascension Island over a period of nineteen years.[1]

Ascension is a small volcanic island in the South Atlantic. On that rocky terrain agriculture is impossible. At the time Marsden went there, three years before the Disaster, the local population managed to raise small kitchen gardens and do some fishing. Ocean traffic had dwindled to emergency calls as air cargo flights took over the task of providing supplies. The main industry of the island was a NATO Air Defense Command base with the best technology for monitoring air traffic and space movement. The base was staffed by one thousand men accompanied by their families. Assignments to Ascension were short-term, not because the island was hazardous, but because the isolation brought hardship to the staff and their families.

The island had taken on a small, permanent dragon colony, which represented a hazard to the population and a definite threat to the military capacity to respond quickly in a crisis. When the Commandant received a letter from Marsden requesting permission to come to the island for a long-term study of the dragons, he was quick to agree. The dragons worried him, though there had been no contact of any kind with them, and he could not spare his own personnel to a dragon

[1] This account of Marsden's time on Ascension has been furnished by Philomel St. James.

study detail. There were very few verminologists in those early days, and he readily overlooked the fact that Marsden had not completed his Ph.D. and came equipped mainly with enthusiasm and a determination to learn dragon language. The facilities of the base and a small space on all supply flights were made available. The ADC gave Marsden detailed maps of the island and helped him find a site for a base camp that was close to the places where they had seen dragons routinely, and that could be reached inconspicuously.

Once his camp was fully equipped, Marsden isolated himself there. The Commandant reluctantly agreed not to fly over him or to send messengers. Marsden allowed himself the luxury of emergency radio contact with the ADC and accepted a jeep for his trips to the base computer banks. He quickly perceived that the island was not merely a routine observation post, as the ADC had assumed, but an active colony with a population twice the ADC estimate, including several young dragons and at least one roil of hatchlings less than a year old. He did not inform the ADC of his finding, fearing they would take steps to eliminate the colony. However, he spotted for them the precise positions that the dragons were likely to defend, and advised them expertly on the best ways to continue peaceful relations.

It took Marsden many years to begin to map out the first rough outline of a grammar of dragon speech. He had to become familiar with the habits of the colony and find where they used their spoken language rather than the percussive. He was forced to rely on long-range listening devices for many years. When he solved the problem of recording conversations among dragons and kits, he was able to begin collecting material. If there had not been a roil with young kits, he realized, he might never have been able even to begin the work he had come to do. After three years he had taught himself to understand the subtleties of the percussive language, but his primary objective was to make direct communication with dragons possible in their own tongue, and of course he was not equipped physically to reproduce the percussive sounds or the bellow. He used the ADC computer to synthesize percussive transmissions, but the dragons did not respond to them. The language itself remained his goal, a long and difficult task. However, he prepared a preliminary lexicon of the percussive language which he sent to Yale as his Ph.D. dissertation project.

Shortly after Marsden sent his thesis to Yale, the Disaster took place in Europe. Marsden was able to prevent any action against the local dragons by the ADC, and familiarity with Marsden may have been responsible for preventing the dragons from attacking the base. Certainly they were very angry. He used the first night of the Disaster as the standard against which he measured all dragon rage. There was peace between the colony and the people on Ascension for two years after the Disaster, but then the Nagata Museum opened and hoard fever broke out all over the world. Within nine months, when the fever was at its height, the dragons took action suddenly, killing every human on Ascension except Marsden, beginning with a devastating raid on the base. He did not know why the dragons had spared him. Familiarity was as close as he could come to a reason. He had lived in their presence for six years, in a kind of mutual tolerance, and alone and unarmed he certainly presented no threat. The dragons allowed one supply plane to land the day after the base had been depopulated, but did not allow the crew to escape. Responding to an emergency call, two planes were dispatched to survey the damage and search for survivors, but the dragons incinerated them in midair. Surveillance of the island had to be carried out from satellites. Marsden was presumed dead.

Marsden, in fact, had not even known that the dragons attacked the base. They had left the colony during the middle of the night, which was unusual, but returned quietly the next afternoon, settling into a regular routine. He did not suspect that there had been trouble until he saw two of the kits pretending to set fire to rocks, making human screams – neither of which they had done before. He went back to his camp and tried without success to raise the base on his radio. He knew then that the worst had happened.

The base was a grisly sight when he got there. The dragons had relied mostly on fire and had been very thorough in their determination to rid the island of humans. They had also destroyed all communications installations. He had to watch, helpless, as they swooped down on the crew of the supply plane and, later that evening, as they demolished the rescue planes. In the end he collected what personal property and papers he could, sorted them by families, and stored them in one of the remaining buildings. Then he collected the bodies, and lit fires of his own. It was a long, arduous task. Years later he gave one account of the attack to the ADC as best he could reconstruct it, drawing on the writing he had done at the time. Once he had made that report, he never referred to the experience again.

He was then a prisoner. The ADC had wisely abandoned any effort to return to the base, so there was no transportation off the island. After dragon-human relations eased, the strategic importance of the Ascension installation had faded with the efficiency of new equipment elsewhere. Marsden's only companions were the dragons. They ignored him for the most part, and he avoided their company for many weeks after the ordeal at the base. Eventually he saw that he had no choice but to go back to the work. They gave him complete freedom of movement and simply pretended not to notice him as he wandered into their groups or sat quietly taking notes or making recordings. As long as he had the equipment, he recorded every noise and every movement. When his supplies ran out, he devised a system combining musical and dance notation to record the percussive language, and made an elaboration of phonic notation so that he could transcribe the full range of sounds used in dragon language. He learned to provide for his basic needs with a minimum of effort and time, taking care to guard his health. He worked constantly, every day. The dragons were his vocation and his recreation. With less complex companions he would likely have gone mad.

St. James says that occasionally his isolation would become oppressive and he would run or shout to work out his anxiety. The worst period culminated one afternoon in the first autumn of his hermitage. He had been falling steadily into a mood of desperate loneliness that she said became suddenly unbearable. He ran wildly, screaming and screaming. Gradually he became aware of the sound of his

V. Philip Marsden and Philomel St. James on a field expedition in Alaska.
Their presence seemed to attract the beasts they sought.
(*Photo: George B. Wharton, Jr*)

screams and came to his senses to find himself surrounded by dragons watching him intently. He never again let himself go completely.

Eventually he had to have supplies to survive, and he returned to the base. He salvaged what he could, mostly materials for his study: recording equipment, writing gear, a little clothing, and some tinned food. The base had an emergency generator powered by a simple solar unit he was able to repair and divert to an undamaged computer. After that his work went more quickly. He lived on Ascension alone for thirteen more years. He was rediscovered by accident during the Third Dragon Census, when dragon-human relations in the world at large, while not cordial, were easier than they had been in the first years after the opening of Nagata.

When the survey team located him in his little camp, Marsden greeted them courteously, but made it clear that he intended to stay on the island until his language studies were complete. The British conceded that he could not be prosecuted under the Non-Intercourse Laws, so he was allowed to stay. The crew insisted on making a return flight to Ascension to bring him supplies. He reluctantly admitted that he had run out of pencils and recording materials and added with a smile that he would love some citrus fruit. He led them back to the ADC field himself, partly because he was enjoying a moment of human companionship, and partly because the kits had assembled and were watching the meeting with growing curiosity and delight.

The rescue plane flew to São Paulo with Marsden's greeting to Froedlich. She was overjoyed to hear from him and packed supplies into one small box: pencils and other writing supplies, a new recording setup, and a dozen oranges. To her dismay the international news media heard about Marsden on Ascension. In spite of her pleading for them to leave him and the dragons alone, an excited group of reporters and cameramen crowded onto the return flight. With grim foreboding Marsden watched them tumble out of the plane at the deserted air base. He traded one full story for a promise of privacy thereafter. The press remained faithful to their promise.

However, several weeks later the Air Defense Command sent a plane to retrieve records and valuables from the base. This flight also brought several requests from Yale, the University of London, and Cambridge University for small, short-term botanical and zoological studies. Since these tasks were not related to the dragons and could be accomplished in his spare time, Marsden was glad to do them and enjoyed recording information outside his normal routine. Word soon got out that he would do high-quality field work free, and subsequent flights brought scores of requests for studies.

He could no longer control the traffic to the island, and, surprisingly, the dragons didn't seem to care who came and went. The ADC had long since given up trying to maintain a base on Ascension, so there were no more official visits to contend with, but the accounts of his isolated life with dragons turned him into an international folk hero. Some of the headlines for these stories were sensational: 'Marsden – Half Man, Half Dragon', 'Boy Orphaned in the Disaster Raised by Dragons on Atlantic Reef'. The London papers carried stories proving that his mother had been raped by a dragon in her New York apartment. At first there were only a few brave souls who rode along on the supply flights. Philomel St. James was one of these. She had wanted to come because she was fascinated by dragons as a subject for drawing. Marsden was glad to have her stay, and they began the association that lasted for the rest of his life.

As time went by, a visit to Ascension became a feat of exploration and adventure. Marsden had limited his supply runs to one every four months, but all sorts of odd craft arrived, by air and on the sea, bearing men and women with recording equipment and what he called 'triumphant expressions'. He had to set up a miniature hospital and became expert in treating exposure and sunburn and in spotting nutritional deficiencies. Finally frustrated in his own work, fearing for the safety of the people who sought him out, and mindful of the sanctity of dragon privacy, he decided to leave the island without completing his study.

He and St. James went to Cananéia to join Froedlich. She had been re-accepted by the University and was able to find room for her old friend to have a study in the library and access to the computer. He received substantial research grants from Information Systems International, Ltd., which allowed him to continue his work. He revised and published his *Lexicon of the Percussive Language of Dragons*, which was the first major publication in verminology. Froedlich and Marsden convinced the *Anatomista Latinoamericano* to accept a series of papers that have become the foundation for modern dragon studies. They worked with St. James, Santander, and Branco until Froedlich's death, five years later.

After Froedlich's death Marsden refused a post at the University of São Paulo and accepted the sponsorship of the North African Semitic League for two return visits to Ascension. The dragon colony was reduced to only two, and he did not find enough new material to justify his continuing the project there. For the next several years he worked as an adviser and as a trouble shooter, negotiating between dragons and their human neighbors. His health broke suddenly during a mission to Hokkaidō and the established colony there, which had begun to harass rural communities near Asahi-dake. He fell during a climb in the higher elevations of the mountain and was severely injured. During his hospitalization in Tōkyō, when it became clear that he would never completely recover, he accepted the offer of Canterbury University to come to Christchurch, New Zealand. Christchurch remained his home for the rest of his life. He established the New Zealand School of Dragon Studies and recruited and trained the next generation to carry on the study of dragon anatomy, behavior, and, of course, language. With the foundation of the School of Dragon Studies, modern verminology began.

Modern Verminology

The School has remained the center for studies in dragon behavior under the guidance of Sean Jones, and for training competent researchers in the complex task of unravelling dragon language under Philomel St. James. (Anatomical studies have moved to Oxford University for the most part, with the departure of Antonia McArdle for England). Whether or not the resources of the School are wasted in trying to construct a 'language' remains an open question. They admit that the problem that lies at the bottom of any study of dragon language remains: finding a dragon who wants to converse. Marsden, Froedlich, Santander, St. James, and Jones are the only people who can be said to have been on intimate terms with dragons. A handful of their students are reported to have had occasional conversations, but verminologists of the current generation are hampered in their efforts to establish the rapport that is fundamental to real communication by the attitude of the beasts themselves. Dragons do not seem to be as curious about people as they once were. If anything, they are more distant and arrogant than they were at the time of the Third Census when Marsden was discovered on Ascension. Therefore, although the urge to speak with this beast on his own terms is very strong, it is no longer clear that the study of his language (even if there is such a language) is to be the most fruitful avenue of exploration for verminologists.

In China, studies have been limited to practical experiments designed to determine what combination of offering and attitude placates a dragon most readily, and to seeking the connection between this and the previous infestations by examining writing from the earlier periods. (See the bibliography published in Beijing).

Predictably, Japanese interests have remained with hoarding because of the Nagata Museum, and because of the large dragon colony to the north of Hokkaidō from which four dragons have made repeated forays in the last sixty years. (See *Nagata Reports*). Mile for mile, Japan has suffered more from dragons than any other country and has shown commendable restraint in dealing with the worms.

After many years a joint Russian–United States project produced the technology that has made the Fourth Census possible and far more accurate than the Third. Canada, principally through the Center at the University of Toronto, has become the verminographics co-ordination point for the world. We will return to this intriguing subject.

The major nations of the world have undoubtedly made vulnerability analyses of scale texture and density, speed-distance acceleration studies, and other attack-related investigations. But the results of these military and intelligence projects have not been made available to civilian verminologists.

The largest research projects have been conducted in the United States, Russia, and in the Sudan on dragon feeding raids. The most productive of these is recorded in a series of publications, *The Dragon, Non-Dragon Interface*, published by the University of Khartoum. The world at large owes a great debt to the University and to the Sudanese government, which have invested in the patient, practical experiments and fostered the ingenuity that has produced screening methods like the Boumani Sonic Net.

Perhaps the most promising recent developments have come from a joint project between Oxford University anatomists and geologists working with Eastman Kodak to modify a new density-scanning technique in which microsound waves are bounced onto a specially modified photographic plate to reveal the internal structure of geological formations. In the next year they will know whether this technique can be sufficiently adapted to permit gross anatomical studies of live dragons. If so, they will have circumvented the previously insurmountable problem of taking specimens for study, and a systematic dragon biology will be possible at last.

The Ominous Implications of Recent Verminographical Research

The study of dragon populations is known as verminographics or geo-verminology. A worldwide network of geo-verminologists is linked to the computer center at the University of Toronto. This center was established ten years ago by interested scholars from Toronto, MIT, and Yale University, who formed the Dragon Survey Group (DSG) with small grants from the US and Canadian governments. Convinced that a new census was vital to an intelligent understanding of the dragon problem, the Group hired two full-time people and began the task of persuading the North American Defense Community that the technology that had been developed here and in the Soviet Union for gathering minutely detailed intelligence information with satellites could be applied to a dragon census. The negotiations proved to be the most difficult part of the entire census project. The Group had to deal with people from the external affairs departments of both the Canadian and US governments, and with the military. Everyone agreed that it would be enormously useful to have specific data on the numbers of dragons present in the world and their actual, rather than their rumored, locations. No one was prepared to admit in public, however, that the sophisticated intelligence technology had been worked out or that satellite observation was in fact routine.

The proposal was buried for two years in the red tape of security matters. When it surfaced again, it was ignored by the NADC, and the Survey Group decided that more drastic measures would have to be tried. Accordingly, they wrote an open letter to the Russian people charging that the Soviets had the technology to pinpoint dragons near population centers before they had become a menace. The letter was delivered to the Embassies in Ottawa and Washington the day after a serious dragon raid in Uzbekistan in which several people had been killed. The letter was never published, of course, but the Soviets demanded to know what was going on. A new phase of negotiations opened, this time involving three governments. Once the Soviets understood the proposal, they supported the Census project vigorously and agreed to co-operate if Soviet personnel could be used to analyze Soviet data. After fourteen months an agreement in principle was reached among the governments. The NADC released satellite observations to the DSG that coincided with known dragon presence so the Survey Group could learn how to recognize dragons in the layout presentation. A team of four Soviets had to be taught the skill. There was another delay while the military of each country came to agreement with the project. A timetable for the actual survey had to be worked out to photograph the entire surface of the planet within a very short time. This meant that the paths of the various satellites had to be co-ordinated without revealing specific information about the routines of these satellites or their capabilities. Once the technology was in place, the entire survey was taken in six days.

We have now, at last, a dragon census that is at least 50 percent accurate. Four factors remain to qualify the complete accuracy of the census: dragons undoubtedly moved about during the six days of the census and may be present in more than one layout; dragons underground do not appear on the layouts; although some dragons in the sea are exposed by their heat if they were near the surface, those beneath the ten-meter level do not appear; even the finest technology cannot record dragons hidden under overhanging projections, or otherwise screened from above. Nevertheless, the census is immensely valuable.

The ominous implications of the results of this survey become clear when a comparison of three maps is made. (These maps and the information in this section are based on research published by the Dragon Survey Group). Over the past seventy years dragon population, or at least visible dragon population, has risen from about 150 or 170 to 1767 at the Fourth Census. While the total number

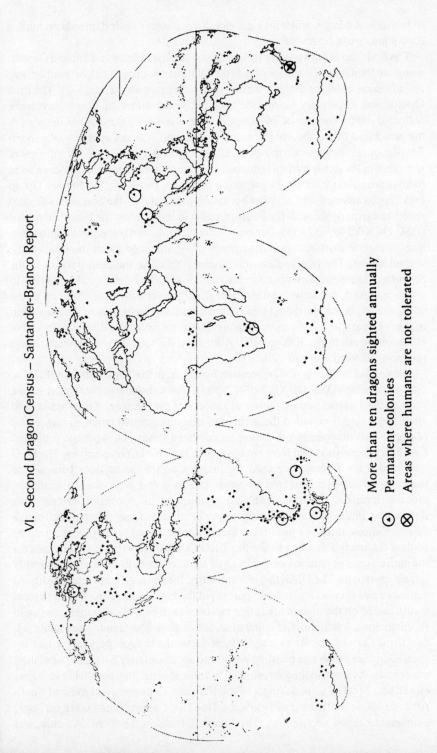

VI. Second Dragon Census – Santander-Branco Report

▸ More than ten dragons sighted annually
⊙ Permanent colonies
⊗ Areas where humans are not tolerated

of beasts is not large, when they are eating voraciously their demands on human food sources can be severe.

The first map is drawn using figures from the First Census and Second Census, using the Santander-Branco report as an additional source. It can be used only as an indication of where dragons were actually seen (see above, pp. 6–7). The First Census was hopelessly inaccurate because it was taken on hearsay evidence collected over a number of years, and no allowances were made for dragons in the sea. In addition, the dragon's ability to mime was not a matter of general knowledge at the time of the census. The Second Census was slightly more reliable, but the time problem remained and figures for dragons in the ocean were hardly more than guesses. In preparing this map, therefore, the Survey Group took these censuses into account but relied primarily on the Santander-Branco report and experience with the Fourth Census in interpreting the historical record (DSG DCXB 3499431=33). The map is drawn to show a reasonable approximation of dragon distribution and numbers of sightings at about the time of the second report. The heaviest concentrations fall below the 50th parallel in the Southern Hemisphere, with colonies east of the Drakensberge Mountains in southern Africa, on Stewart Island, and along the west coast of Chile up to the 40th parallel. In the Northern Hemisphere a similar pattern occurs: the area north of the 50th parallel has the most dragons. There are isolated individuals in higher elevations south to the 30th parallel. Altogether the total dragon population was probably between 150 and 170.

The second map (opposite) represents figures from the Third Census with some major revisions (DSG DCXB 3499779=84). The census was completed in one year, so the Dragon Survey Group assumed that the number of dragons missed altogether roughly equalled the number of dragons counted twice, giving a total of about 340 dragons in all. Using an educated hindsight, we have projected figures for those areas that were not covered in the Third Census survey. The DSG disregarded the figures they used for dragons on the ocean floor because the census used samples gathered by sonar facilities that were readily available, around Bermuda, off Mauritius, and in the area of Ascension (where they discovered Philip Marsden during the collection process). Preparing for the Fourth Census, the DSG used these locations and added seven others. In doing so they discovered that by chance the Third Census had extrapolated figures for the entire ocean population on the basis of samples taken in areas with unusually large populations. The DSG, therefore, omitted the census figures and substituted a number that seemed logical – 15 percent of the land population. The 15 percent is distributed on the map in areas that can be shown by oceanographic survey to be anomalous, having higher concentrations of flora and fauna. Thus modified, the Third Census reveals two significant facts: the dragon population had increased by more than one hundred percent to approximately 340, and population concentrations were no longer restricted to areas near the 50th parallel or in higher elevations. Most of Canada, most of the Eurasian Continent, and most of South America above 300 meters or below the Tropic of Capricorn had taken on large, permanent dragon populations. The Faeroe Islands in the North Atlantic, and

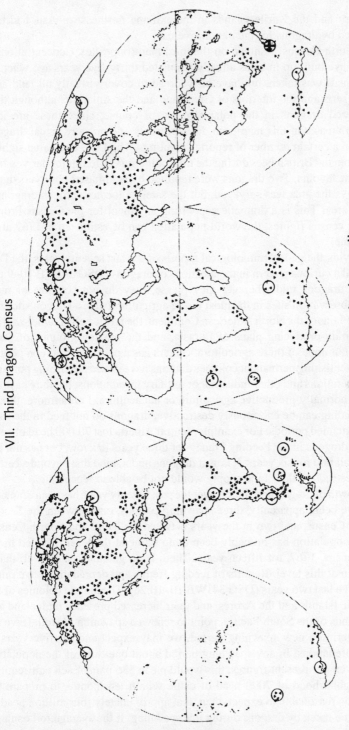

VII. Third Dragon Census

▴ More than ten dragons sighted annually
⊙ Permanent colonies
⊗ Areas where humans are not tolerated

Paramushir and the Kurile Islands in the extreme northeast of Asia had been confiscated by dragons for their exclusive use.

The Fourth Census is shown on the third map (opposite). Concentrations of dragons have built up in areas already populated thirty-five years ago when the Third Census was taken, but have also spread to cover virtually all land areas except deserts and the interiors of Greenland and the Antarctic, although there are scattered dragons in the polar regions, of course, since these are ideal recreation areas. On this map each dot represents one or more actual dragons, rather than a certain number of reported sightings. The DSG compared sighting reports from the British Isles during the time of the survey to figures derived from the satellite layouts. Two dragons were reported by land-based observers during the six days the area was surveyed, but the satellite located thirteen dragons in the same area. This is a dramatic supporting argument for the Census Project. Using the census figures, the world population can be estimated at 1767 at the present time.

In studying the geo-verminological reports of the last seventy years, the DSG discovered a curious pattern in the locations of dragons (DSG 34JWB 10–9:67). Although dragons raid wherever they please, they do not colonize or make habitual observation sites in the most fertile agricultural areas. Dragon sites ring the Great Plains of the North American Continent, the fertile belt of middle Africa, the vast grain-producing plans of Eurasia, and the grazing grounds of South America, but none of these agricultural centers has a permanent dragon population. In establishing permanent colonies dragons have destroyed fishing ports and mining operations and other industrial or military installations, but they have not disrupted normally productive agriculture or aquaculture. Furthermore, though dragon feeding can be enormously destructive, dragons do not feed in the same area for extended periods. For example, central Alberta lost 70,000 head of cattle to mating dragons in the Feeding Frenzy for three years in a row, but has not had even a small raid for six years. It is as if dragons understood that beyond a certain level of destruction their food supply would not be able to regenerate.

The growth of dragon population over the past seventy years has been dramatic. There have been, apparently, three spawning periods, one between the Second and Third Census, and two in the years between the Third and Fourth Census. The total population has probably been quite stable at the level revealed in the Fourth Census, 1767, for fifteen years. There is no guarantee, however, that it will remain at this level. Reports of feeding frenzy and depredation have quadrupled in the last two years (DSG 34JWB 10–10:26). The dragon colonies of the Cape Verde Islands and the Azores, and their increased presence on Iceland and on the islands of the South Pacific, point to renewed spawning as well. If we are in fact entering a new spawning period, we may expect another five years of severe depredations. In any spawning period about one-third of the population mates. Given our present figures, this would mean 586 pairs. Each pair requires in the neighborhood of 7000 head of cattle within ten months to prepare for mating. It is reasonable to expect, then, that approximately four million head of cattle will be taken by dragons during this spawning. If the average roil contains

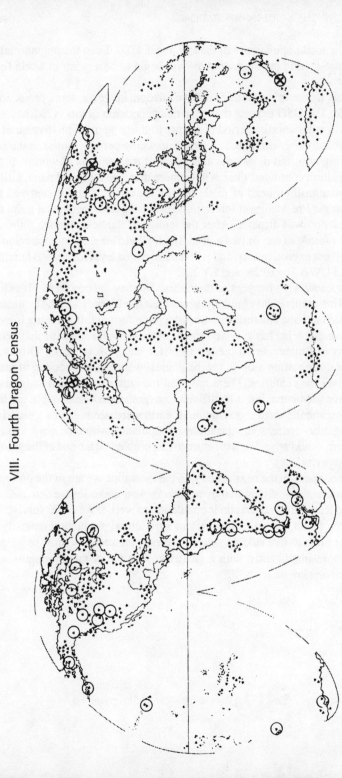

VIII. Fourth Dragon Census

▲   One or more dragons present during survey

◉   Permanent colonies

⊗   Areas where humans are not tolerated

seven kits, the total population will then be about 4700. Even feeding normally, without the pre-mating pressure, dragons will begin to be a factor in world food supplies.

Beyond this we are in the area of pure speculation; however, some projections may be made. The DSG expects that once this generation of kits is hatched and grown we will enter another period of twenty to thirty years of relative quiet. It seems likely that there will then be another spawning period, similar to the one we are entering now, but more critical because of the numbers of worms. If the established pattern continues, there will be more than one thousand pairs, killing better than nine million head of cattle for the spawning. Careful study of the material from the Pre-Medieval Infestation Period suggests that at that point the dragon population will disperse. After the middle of the next century sightings will dwindle rapidly to one or two a year. The total visible dragon population of the world will not exceed twenty, and will remain at that level for several hundred years (DSG 34JWB 10=10:28, and LY 22).

We do not know what happens to them then. Do they destroy themselves like lemmings? This seems highly unlikely, given their intelligence and the testimony Marsden is said to have collected from his dragon informant. If the latter is even marginally correct, Vlad has survived scores of these cycles. Perhaps they retire to the oceans and hibernate on the sea floor for hundreds of years. This is an attractive idea, suggesting a cause for the gradual warming and cooling of areas in the seas over the centuries. There has been the rather sensational suggestion that they leave the planet, but it is difficult to hypothesize a reasonable method for them to escape the earth's gravitation. If earth were one breeding ground on a regular migratory route, some questions of population would be answered but hundreds more would arise. We will return to this problem at the end of the second section, 'Longevity'.

Whatever happens in the next century, in the meantime we are in the presence of greedy and increasingly numerous neighbors who make severe demands on our ability to feed ourselves and their population as well. If we are to survive the next spawning intact, we must increase our agricultural production radically. If we are to continue to live side by side with these creatures, we must be able to meet them more intelligently, with a greater knowledge of their strengths and, perhaps, their weaknesses.

Part II

ANATOMICAL AND BEHAVIORAL CHARACTERISTICS

Physical Description

A discussion of dragons themselves has to start with their size and appearance, even though photographs of dragons are commonplace. They are, before anything else, impressively large, and pictures do not convey the full impression of their majestic and sinuous bulk. The mature dragon is typically between 20 and 30 meters in length and has a wingspan of from 15 to 24 meters, though there are unsubstantiated reports of dragons close to 46 meters in length. They are basically winged snakes – the head scarcely larger in diameter than the neck, with an elongated body, which tapers slightly to the long tail. They are able to compress their bodies by as much as one-quarter, rather like the earthworm. In compression the whole body from just behind the head to the end of the tail becomes wider, in part from the compression itself, and in part from the erection of the scales, which stand away from the body. This compression is used in two ways. On the ground it is a challenge gesture, the wings spread and cupped forward and the collar erect. In the air it is more playful, accompanied by rapid, looping flight interspersed with bursts of speed and sudden reversals in direction and altitude (Froedlich, ABD, 93).

Though small when hatched, anywhere from 34 to 60 centimeters, kits multiply in length in the first days of life and continue to grow rapidly, attaining 9 to 15 meters in the first year (Grenner and Del Rio, RevZoo 14:7:4). In Marsden's study of the dragon colony on Ascension, two-thirds of the roil he observed when he first arrived continued to grow in length and height, as well as in overall bulk, for several years beyond metabolic maturity. The largest in this group of eight was 28 meters, the smallest 19 meters, with the remaining six ranging between 22 and 25 meters. The deviations in growth and size cannot be attributed to sex, apparently, since both sexes are represented equally throughout the spectrum in all samples collected to date (Froedlich, ABD, 143).

Dragons do not discriminate among themselves in matters of size, though mated dragons are usually close to the same length. Marsden was unable to account for variation in size from the information he collected on Ascension, and no subsequent studies have remedied this gap satisfactorily. In the ninth year of his stay on Ascension Marsden located a roil two days after hatching. He observed this hatch until the time he left, and they followed the same pattern of size inconsistency that he had observed in the first roil.

30

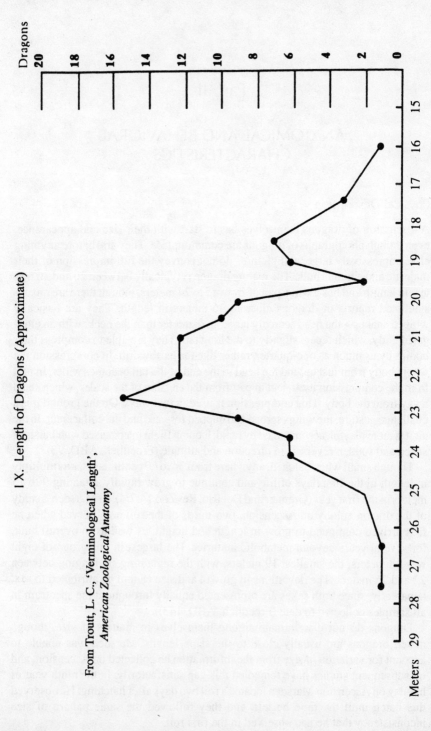

IX. Length of Dragons (Approximate)

From Troutt, L. C., 'Verminological Length',
American Zoological Anatomy

Others after Marsden have speculated on the causes for the wide variation in size. Troutt attributes it to uneven nourishment of the prenatal kit (ZR 43:8). Steinmetz suggests that insufficient shell thickness exposes some unborn kits to excessive heat, impairing their ability to grow rapidly during the time when they must depend on non-dragon digestion (Steinmetz, CompAnat CLV1:4); Glaumer, in one of his more speculative moods, suggests that small dragons are predestined for cold habitats, or areas with meager food supplies, the variation in size thereby assuring even population distribution (Glaumer, *Book of Beasts*, 4–10). The latter suggestion raises more problems than it solves, but in fact there is at present no way to test any of these hypotheses. It seems reasonable to assume that these creatures, who display such variety in color, temperament, and behavior, also vary in size randomly, within a range that makes them easily the largest creatures extant.

Although they are enormous animals, the largest since the extinction of the great dinosaurs, they are able to fit themselves into surprisingly small spaces. They are rather like cats in this ability. A storehouse thought safely secured against raids can be broached through an opening scarcely larger than a dragon head. This is due to the flexibility of the skeletal structure, which can bend at every point like a snake's, and to the absence of large muscle clusters. The widest immovable part of the anatomy is the skeletal housing for the fire chamber. Since the wings and forelegs can be carried before or behind the chamber, dragons require a comparatively small opening to negotiate their full diameter (Froedlich, ABD, 95). They prefer not to squeeze through narrow holes, however, which is not surprising in an animal that seeks comfort and dignity. However, a fold of pregnant sheep or a bit of treasure can lure a hungry or lustful dragon through an opening as small as 1.2 by 2.4 meters. Thus, a dragon could not get into a typical Canadian tract house by the front door, but he could curl his entire length into the elevator of a large metropolitan department store.

The head is approximately one-eighth of the full length of the dragon, the muzzle tapered, the cranium rising to a rounded brow, continuing in an elongated bulging dome. Compared to the human head with its high, round crown, the dragon head is long and sleek, not appreciably larger in diameter than the neck when it is compared to the human ball-on-a-string style of anatomy. However, there is sufficient capacity for the cerebral hemispheres and a large cerebellum, which are likely larger in proportion to the rest of the brain than that of the human. This is conjecture, of course (see Plate X). Charred fragments of dragon skulls have been found, but no complete skull has been recovered to date. Since no dragon specimen has been taken alive and intact, vivisection has been precluded. Given their intelligence, their unerring sense of balance, and the abnormally long skull, the enlargement of both the cerebral hemispheres and the cerebellum seems a reasonable assumption. This does not of itself substantiate the NZSDS assumption of superior cognitive activity, of course.

The length of the muzzle from nostril to eye socket is roughly one-third the length of the head. The nostrils are wide and flare to expel smoke or fire. The mouth opens the full length of the muzzle. There is a single row of sixty-four

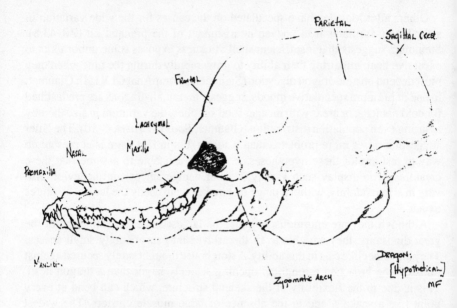

X. Comparison of Dragon with Human and Canine Skulls

large, long, strongly tapered teeth. The incisors are sharply pointed and adapted to tearing. The prominent canines can be up to 80 centimeters long and are never covered even when the jaws are closed (Froedlich, ABD, 33). Examination of drawings from the period of the Pre-Medieval Infestation suggests that the teeth were often mistaken for chin whiskers. The tongue can be extended and curled laterally to form a tube to direct the fire. The eyes are lidded, often set under a bony ridge. The pupils are vertical ovals set in deep yellow or silver irises, strongly marked with red or green. The eyes are controlled independently and can be focused forward or directed to the sides to observe a full 300 degrees.

The legs are long and thin, flagged from the chest wall to the heel with a webbing similar to that of the collar. Both pairs of feet are heavily armored with scales. The toes are long and flexible, armed with sturdy claws, which they sharpen on rocks. Dragons have strong opposable thumbs on fore and hind feet. Ordinarily they bear the weight of their bodies on the heels, leaving the toes free for grasping. On occasion they can rise on their toes and move very swiftly in a headlong trot, advancing both legs on the same side of the body in concert. However, on the ground they prefer to move slowly, resting more of their length on the surface, propelling themselves forward by a modification of the serpentine movement: that is, they let their legs trail close to their sides and push against any available obstacle with whatever portion of the body is in contact, using the tail or toes for assistance or added speed (Froedlich, ABD, 89). The wide trail of underbrush crushed by a slithering dragon is a welcome sight to a verminologist on a stalking expedition.

Measurements of the tracks of running adult dragons indicate that dragons are

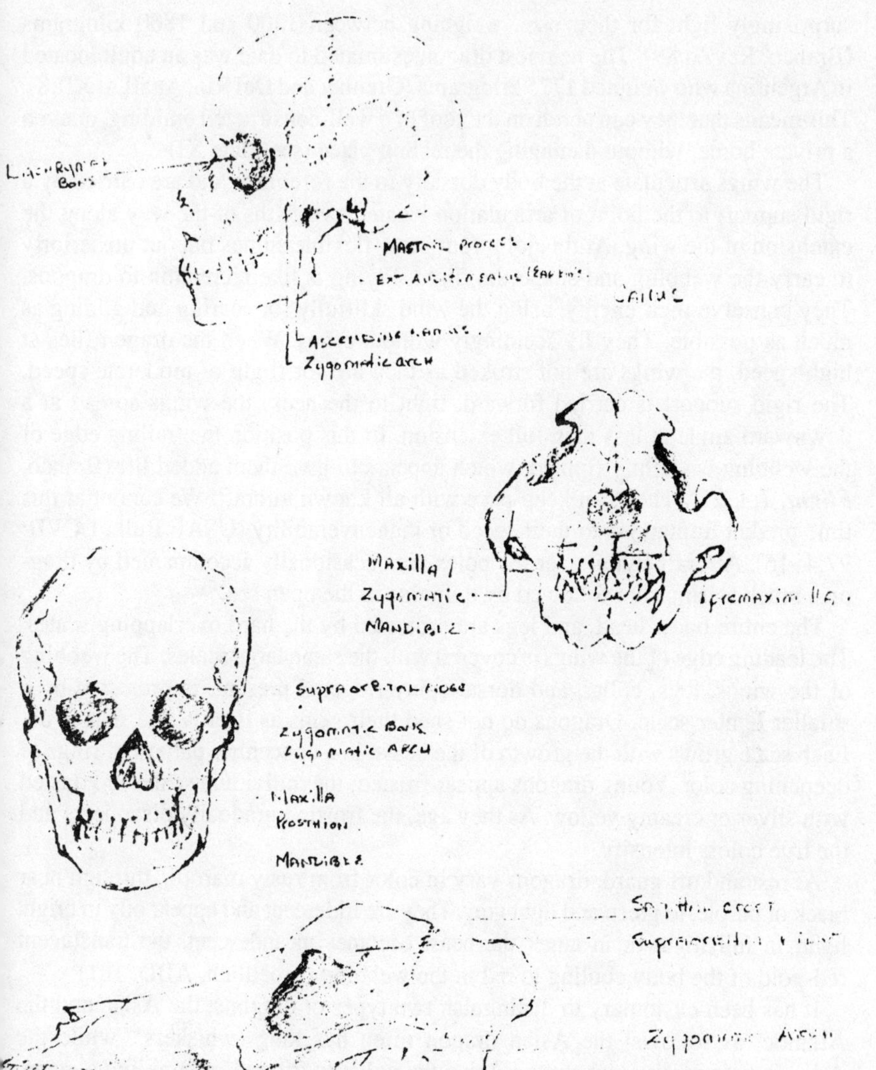

LACHRYMAL
BONE

MASTOID PROCESS

EXT. AUDITIA SALUS (EAR HOLE)

SALUS

ASCENDING RAMUS.

ZYGOMATIC ARCH

MAXILLA /

ZYGOMATIC

MANDIBLE

PREMAXILLE.

SUPRAORBITAL RIDGE

ZYGOMATIC BONE

ZYGOMATIC ARCH

MAXILLA

PROSTHION

MANDIBLE

SAGITTAL CREST

SUPRAORBITAL RIDGE

ZYGOMATIC ARCH

CANUS

NF AFTER CORNWALL.

surprisingly light for their size, weighing between 1200 and 1800 kilograms (Branco, RevZo 89). The heaviest dragon estimated to date was an adult located in Argentina who weighed 1775 kilograms (Grenner and Del Rio, AnatLat XII:8). This means that they can perch on the roof of a well-constructed building, or even a private home, without damaging the resting place (see Plate XI).

The wings articulate at the body dorsally to the forelimbs and are carried by a rigid support to the point of articulation located two-fifths of the way along the extension of the wing. At this joint four semi-flexible spines fan out posteriorly to carry the webbing and shape the flight. Flying is like recreation to dragons. They conserve their energy, using the wind skillfully for soaring and gliding as much as possible. They fly seemingly without effort. When the dragon flies at high speed, the wings are not stroked as they are for flight of moderate speed. The rigid support is carried forward, tight to the neck, the wings spread at a downward angle at less than full extension. In this position the trailing edge of the webbing is slightly rippled, which appears to give them added lift (Branco, *Flight*, 7:3, 21). They can keep pace with all known aircraft. We cannot at this time predict limitations to their speed or maneuverability (USAF Bull., LCVII: 97:4–16). Aircraft flying over the poles are occasionally accompanied by dragons, much as ships are followed by dolphins in the open sea.

The entire body, head, and legs are protected by the hard overlapping scales. The leading edge of the wings is covered with the same large scales. The webbing of the wings, legs, collar, and dorsal spiny ridge, if present, is protected by a smaller lighter scale. Dragons do not shed their skins as lizards and snakes do. Each scale grows with the growth of the beast, in a concentric pattern of rings of deepening color. Young dragons appear frosted; the individual scales are dusted with silver or creamy yellow. As they age, the frosting gradually disappears and the true colors intensify.

At rest and off guard, dragons vary in color from rusty maroon, through near black or purple, to green and light grey. They are iridescent and appear oily in bright light. In full flight or in anger the beast becomes incandescent, the translucent red-gold of the body cooling to red in the webbing (Froedlich, ABD, 101).

It has been customary to distinguish two types of dragons, the Asian and the Atlantic, as follows: the Asian dragon often has long 'whiskers', while the Atlantic type rarely does. In the Asian the collar is fringed, resembling a mane, while in the Atlantic the collar is most typically a uniform, solid webbing carried close to the neck except when the animal is excited. The tail terminates in a fringe in the Asian type and in a spade shape in the Atlantic. The Asian dragon is more often 'horned' with kobs or hornlike protrusions of scales as part of the collar or just above the eyes. There is an emerging unanimity in the verminological community that these are in fact not two distinct species or even breeds. Certainly there are enormous variations in size, color, and configuration in each group, so that a horned, maned dragon may have a spade tail, and a dragon who conforms exactly to the Atlantic type may have two or even three horns. In other words, dragons of all appearances belong to a single, highly various species (Branco, ZooJ XIV: 19).

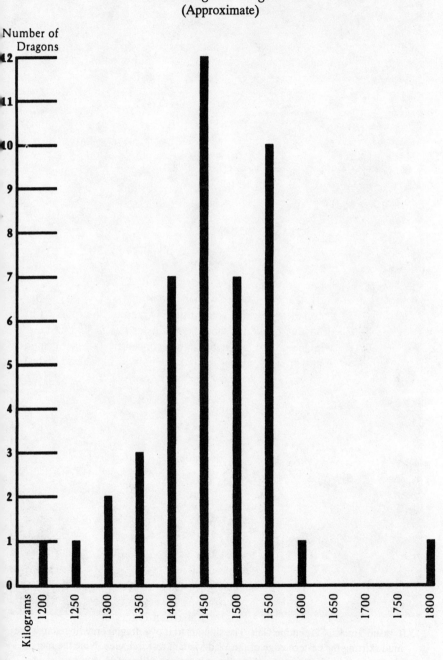

XI. Weight of Dragons
(Approximate)

From Troutt, L. C. 'Verminological Weight',
American Zoological Anatomy.

XII. Mud Tracks: Serpentine Gait. The sinuous trail of a dragon crawling across the mud skirting the eastern edge of the Wad Madani research area. Note the marks left by the wings touching the soft surface. (*Photo: M. Halib*)

The Mime

Dragons are reputed to be shape-changers by the traditions from previous infestations (LY 6). This ability is difficult to substantiate or assess since if it were a characteristic in fact, the dragon would appear to the investigator in the altered shape. The investigator would not know that he was observing a disguise unless he had watched the dragon change, and there are no responsible reports of this process. Until there is hard evidence that they can indeed alter their forms, it is reasonable to attribute this particular tradition to the awe dragons inspire in their neighbors.

Although they do not seem to be able to assume the appearance of an object that is not in the immediate vicinity, it is certainly true that they can assume the color, texture, and general appearance of their surroundings in what is called 'the mime'. This sophisticated elaboration of the chameleon's disguise allows dragons to take recreation by camouflaging themselves near human settlements, observing the daily routine unwittingly performed in their presence. Infrared transmissions recorded from weather and observation satellites reveal dragons clearly in areas where no sightings have been reported. The Fourth Census, using this technology, proved that dragons are more nearly ubiquitous than is commonly thought. It is likely that people who cannot remember ever having seen a dragon have themselves been seen by dragons (DSG DCXB 3488742).

As he assumes the mime, the dragon appears to melt away before the unblinking eye. The collar and the projections down the spine disappear first. Gradually the entire beast seems to disappear, replaced by the background scene. Dragons can reproduce natural or manmade objects, or combinations of either, with ease. Observers on opposite sides of a miming dragon will see each other as if through the beast (Jones, NZJV 4:17). There are clues, however. The sharp, suspicious eye can detect the characteristic outline imposed upon the natural scene. The mime looks more distinct or more 'real' than the original, like a perfectly focused projection of an old Kodachrome slide. Unusual heat is another clue, or an expected warm breeze or radiance, which cannot be attributed to a logical source. Often there is a trace of dragon stench, that unique odor of scorching iron, phosphorous, and charcoal. The eyes remain unchanged, and a transposition will occur if the dragon moves, as it takes a minute or two for the illusion to form. The mime is often given away by heat in winter (Froedlich, ABD, 101). The dragons who watched the Colorado ski resort in Crested Butte assumed the mime on the slopes. Skiers on the lifts were treated to a view of two dragon-shaped puddles of melting snow and ice spilling over, forming small streams freezing down the mountainside (*Rocky Mountain News*).

The mime is retained through low-level exertions. It makes undetected foraging easy, as the prey disappears into the illusion (DNDI:TDD 14). In mime they can converse percussively without betraying their presence, and can crawl slowly overground, shifting the disguise as they go. The mime makes them virtually invisible in the water, for they can swim almost without effort, so the mime can be maintained at moderate speeds over long distances. Only the eyes show, floating through the sea unblinking. Infrared scanners are necessary for finding any dragon in water deep enough to cover him (Jones, NZSDSWP 20). On land, if they must move quickly, or if they become angry or excited or even very happy, the mime is destroyed.

Dragons use their mimic abilities to augment stealth. They do not automatically assume the appearance of their surroundings as chameleons do. If it is useful to them to disappear, they do so. But if they do not care if they are seen, or if they disdain their stalkers, they do not bother to assume the mime, but proceed as it pleases them in defiance of their hunters (DNDI:TDD 15).

Metabolism

Two of the important questions that plagued verminology in the early stage were 'Why do dragons breathe fire?' and 'How do they produce their enormous heat?' Both questions are linked to metabolism. A breakthrough in understanding dragon metabolism came when Marsden took up Froedlich's speculation that fire and the prolonged periods of fasting had to be related to an unusual digestive process. She supplied him with the notes from her observations of dragon feeding habits collected on the Taitao trip, and with the preliminary work she had done on precisely these two questions. He worked in private on the project for several years, finally completing his presentation after he returned from Ascension, and consulted with her and Santander. Later this paper was read by his assistant, St. James, at the Fifty-eighth Congress of Anatomists in Rome, where it created a storm of disbelief. Here is a description of that paper as it appeared in the program for that convention (58th ICA, Rome, *Program*):

> MARSDEN, P., and SANTANDER, B. (read by P. St. James) 'Dragon Metabolism'. The dragon digests his meal rapidly, in a process not dissimilar to mammalian digestion with one vital difference: once the food is thoroughly mixed with the gastric juices, it is not broken down into digestible form and transferred to the bloodstream through the length of a digestive tract. It is transferred to the second stomach, which lies anterior to the heart along the ventral surface of the spine. It can be stored in this stomach for an indefinite time. As need arises, tiny amounts are drawn forward to the fire chamber where, by the process unique to this animal, it is broken down into sub-molecular particles and recombined into true dragon food. The byproduct of this process is heat on a vast scale. The newly created dragon food is combined in the form of steam with the steam of the bloodstream and then is circulated throughout the system. There is no waste, and therefore no excretory process.

Since that initial presentation this theory has been accepted as the best explanation for the peculiarities of dragon metabolism, and will undoubtedly stand until vivisection or its equivalent is possible.

XIII. A dragon assuming the mime. This remarkable photograph is a detail from one
frame of the record made by the survey team in the Cascades (see p. 55).
It shows the tail taking on the appearance of course sand and pebbles, matching
exactly the terrain of the observation site. Note that the extremity changes
faster than the main structure of the tail. (*Photo: P. D. Cohen*)

The uniquely efficient metabolic system allows the dragon to eat almost at will,
storing quantities of food sufficient to last for years, even decades, of fasting. A
light meal – a goat, for instance – can sustain a mature dragon for several days,
though hard figures are difficult to obtain.

Body Temperature

Dragon blood, that potent ingredient in folk medicine, serves a double purpose:
first, as a conveyor of energy as explained above, and second, as an efficient
coolant. According to the Froedlich-Marsden theory, the heart pumps blood in
the form of steam through the entire body swiftly, but the vessels in the tail and
in the webbing of the wings and legs are smaller, slowing the flow and allowing
the blood to cool rapidly. This, in turn, decreases the volume of the blood,

allowing the free-flowing to continue in spite of the constriction of the vessels. Cooled, the blood returns to the channels in the interior of the body, where it gathers heat as it runs past the bones with their characteristic fire channels, until it is steaming by the time it passes over the fire chamber again (Froedlich, ABD, 174). This vital cooling function explains why an angry dragon rises to fly – he must cool his blood in the spreading wings. If there were no such thermal control, a dragon would burn in the heat of his own anger. If a dragon could be killed at the height of his metabolic rage, he would be his own pyre. This is another reason why so few dragon remains are found.

When the dragon is at rest or contented, the body temperature is lower, and no special cooling in the webbing is needed to maintain proper thermal balance. According to this theory, during prolonged flights in the upper atmosphere, or, it is speculated, in space, the dragon would not need to take in additional water, in spite of his high metabolic rate, as the frigid conditions would provide sufficient external cooling to prevent excessive water loss. During these flights the heartbeat would drop to the level of normal waking activity, even though the heat produced would be intense (Froedlich, ABD, 101).

A dragon profoundly asleep in what is misnamed the 'coma' is estimated to have a skin temperature of 43 to 55 degrees C, depending upon age. This in itself is sufficient to disprove the old classification of dragons with the giant lizards, cold-blooded animals. As the dragon's activity increases, his metabolic rate increases also. Fully active dragons radiate enough heat to distort the air around them, which makes them difficult targets, even for photography, and gives their movements a shimmer that is both attractive and hypnotic. They are ideal subjects for thermography, of course, and it is this tool that has made the Froedlich/ Marsden metabolic theory so widely accepted, in spite of the reluctance of the scientific community to consider so radical a physical-chemical process possible in a life form (58th Du Forêt ICA, Paris, *Proceedings*).

No mature dragon eats raw meat on land, as all his food is automatically cooked before he swallows it. A dragon in full flight or a thoroughly angry dragon spouts flame, as the media are keen to point out. The flame is caused by the rapid metabolic rate, which pushes excessive heat forward through the mouth and nostrils, where it is concentrated before it is expelled. If the rate is high enough, the heat of his rage ignites the air about his head. No angry dragon can be killed easily by conventional means since the intensity of his heat impairs the efficiency of the guidance system of any weapon as it approaches within a meter of the body, or upward of seven meters about the head (RCMP Advisory Bulletin 431J XP 117). Tales of dragon slaying from the Pre-Medieval Infestation period refer to very young dragons, who do not acquire their full fire power until just prior to maturity, or occasionally to sleeping or unwary dragons. The chances of catching a dragon asleep or off guard are minute, of course.

Respiration

The term 'fire-breathing dragon' is, in fact, an inaccurate description of the beast. The answer to the question 'Why do dragons breathe fire?' is 'They don't.' Dragons do not breathe at all in the sense of respiration, once they are full-grown, as all their metabolic needs are supplied by the processes of the fire chamber. Thus they are not bound to an oxygen atmosphere and can range at will under water or, theoretically, in space. However, the nostrils and mouth do provide air passages to the interior, serving as cooling vents, circulating superheated air to the outside. On contact with the oxygen atmosphere, this heat ignites any flammable material present in the air, as indicated above, and gives the appearance of fire breathing (Froedlich, ABD, 173).

Until the dragon kit is fully mature, he digests his food in the conventional manner and respires, taking in oxygen and expelling carbon dioxide. As the kit matures, the spongy structure of the lungs atrophies, leaving sacs of six to ten chambers with a total capacity half again that of an adult human male (Froedlich, ABD, 252). In the maturation process the bones acquire their characteristic fire channels as the kit develops the ability to reassemble the atomic matter of his food. This dependency on ordinary respiration and digestion makes the young vulnerable to attack by predators and confines them to temperate climates in an oxygen-rich atmosphere (Grenner and Del Rio, RevZoo 14:7:4).

Feeding

The ideal situation for Wandering dragons in a normal feeding pattern on land is an observation post in an unpopulated area, at a high altitude with an unobstructed view on three sides, within easy flying distance of other dragons, close to unguarded pastures (preferably beef or sheep, though other meat will be tolerated), and close to a ready supply of fresh or salt water. They also situate themselves near grazing areas for wild ruminants – moose, caribou, wildebeest, and so forth. It is this selection of site that gives the Fourth Census map the characteristic rings around the great grazing lands of the world. Given these ideal conditions, a dragon will eat once every five to ten days. Because of the efficient metabolism, dragons do not require as much raw fuel as would animals of comparable size with a more conventional digestive system. However, they are large and do make demands on available food supplies. A single animal may be taken, or if it is small or if the dragon is particular about which portions he will eat, two or three may be butchered. If he has to travel longer distances for food, he will eat more to save himself the trouble of feeding more frequently (Froedlich, ABD, 8).

The heat produced by the metabolism requires that the dragon drink at will. If he is at rest or in Observation, he does not dehydrate, but if he is active, he must replenish his water supply often. Dragons drink water by sucking through the

XIV. Mating dragons turn peaceful Lead Pond into steam. Although the centrarchid and cyprinid fish populations of this small Adirondack pond survived, the salmonid fishes were destroyed by the drastic change in water temperature.
(*Photo: Bruce Byrne*)

rolled tongue. They do not lap at it as dogs do. Apparently they can also drink by letting the water flow into the opened throat. They have been observed swimming slowly across the surface of the ocean, letting their momentum push the water down their throats, swallowing only occasionally (Jones, NZSDSWP 15). They prefer the salinity of the open sea, but will drink fresh water, reducing ponds and even small lakes to a muddy residue. They will not touch stagnant or heavily polluted water (Froedlich, ABD, 15).

Interestingly, dragons enjoy vegetation fully as much as meat or fish, and revel in the abundance of seaweeds that they can eat without scorching. Sargasso is a particular favorite of females during the retreat. They do not hesitate to include fishes or sailors in the salad if any are at hand (Jones, CSN 57:42).

We know very little about the feeding habits of dragons in the oceans. The University of Tōkyō is conducting a long-term study of fluctuations in fish populations in the Sea of Okhotsk, and Stephansky is conducting a similar study in the Tasman Sea for the University of Auckland, but no conclusive evidence to date links dragons to any depletion of fish populations. Apparently they do not currently present a serious threat to the supply of marine food available for human consumption (Houbek, *Verminous Depletion of Marine Fauna*, 187).

Over the years our problems with dragons have not arisen from their presence in the oceans, nor even from hoarding, once we learned not to expect to be enriched by dragon booty. Dragons are a problem, and an increasingly serious problem, because they harvest supplies of red meat grown for human consumption. The livestock ranges of the world are the dragon's grazing grounds. Dragon raids have joined the list of perils the modern farmer must expect, and the dragon-culling of newborn stock and their cows is a routine part of cattle breeding, even in the larger operations where most activity is kept indoors.

The plundering dragon, eating voraciously without attention to what or where he eats, is a rarity, although this is the stereotype of dragon feeding. Such a dragon is either freshly awakened from a prolonged rest (in which case the initial feeding will be the only indiscriminate meal) or else is preparing for the great mating flight. The postpartum female is a special category restricted solely to the ocean (viz. Jones, NZSDSWP 12, 15, 10). Of these special conditions, the mating orgy is the most destructive. A dragon preparing for mating, male or female, must take in at least two metric tons of food each twenty-four hours over a period of two to three weeks, depending upon the availability of food. A rest period of a week to ten days follows, and the cycle is repeated until the dragon is fully satiated. Upward of 3500 cattle may be killed and eaten in the pre-mating period. The dragon is then ready to enter a long fast. The 'depredations of dragons' recorded in the Eurasian folk history can be attributed to this phenomenon (LY 11).

A thorough investigation of the problem of shared red meat supplies is being conducted by the University of Khartoum, supported by the North African Semitic League. Results of this ongoing research are published as they become available in *The Dragon, Non-Dragon Interface: A Study in Ingestive Preference* and *Techniques of Defense and Deterrent* (University of Khartoum). Since this is the area where humans must compete with dragons, a detailed summary of the research to date is presented here.

The University established two research sites. The first, near Wad Madani on the Nile, is a control site. A small cottage was built and equipped with surveillance equipment and living facilities. During the initial study a large herd of Hereford-Brahma hybrid cattle was kept on open grazing land. No attempt was made to interfere with the normal feeding habits of the dragons attracted to the site by the high-quality, easy prey. The task of the researchers was to observe and record every movement of dragons in the test area.

The initial study lasted forty months. Eight dragons visited the area. They were named according to the order of their appearance, and individual records were maintained on each one, noting the time of day, the approach, the kill, the number of prey taken, and the kind of meal. Since other animals were killed in the neighborhood of the Wad Madani site, the cattle killed at the feeding station were not the only source of food for the dragons involved (DNDI:SIP 7).

During the first thirty-seven months of the study, six dragons ate at the test area, four regularly and two occasionally. During this period the dragons killed 169 cattle, a kill rate of 4.5 per month. At this rate the herd, which included fertile cows, maintained its population in spite of the dragons' particular preference for pregnant prey. In the thirty-eighth month one of the regular visitors, #6, fell into the pre-mating feeding pattern. He was joined by a mated pair, #7 and #8. The dragons who had been regular visitors did not reappear after the pre-mating dragons began to raid the herd (DNDI:SIP 12). The study had to be terminated at the end of the fortieth month because of the depletion of the herd. A new control study will begin this year, and other feed animals will be introduced: water buffalo, sheep, goats, and pigs as well as cattle.

Based on their observations, the Interface team distinguishes four basic dragon hunting patterns.

I   Stoop Pattern. This is the usual approach for a meal in daylight. Dragon approaches in flight, circles above herd, selecting prey. May stampede herd and cut choice from herd. Drops suddenly, striking neck or mid-back. Occasionally dismembers in same action that kills. Settles to eat.

II   Stealth Pattern. Used principally at night or in dim light. Approaches in mime, crawling along ground or waits in mime for herd to approach. Herd usually unaware of presence. Strikes suddenly: usual target, hind legs.

III Double Killing. Either Stoop or Stealth pattern used for initial kill. Second and all subsequent on Stoop Pattern. May make all kills before eating, or may kill and eat sequentially.

IV   Feeding Frenzy. Ninety percent are airborne strikes. Twenty-three percent never touch ground at all. Kill and eat indiscriminately.

During the feeding run in the Frenzy Pattern, the dragon eats in the air, scooping up his prey and devouring it as he turns to make another pass over the herd. He may co-operate with his mate or another dragon and herd the frightened animals into a fence corner or canyon and systematically eat every one, sometimes without bothering to kill first. He eats the whole animal, or as much of it as he can cram in before taking the next (DNDI:SIP 9, 12).

In the last three months of the study three dragons feeding in the Frenzy Pattern killed 254 cattle in 30 raids. In other words, 60 percent of all kills were made in approximately 18 percent of the raids in 7.5 percent of the total time of the study. In the single most destructive raid three dragons ate 16 cattle in the space of 12 minutes (DNDI:SIP 12).

By examining the carcasses after each kill, the Interface researchers were able to classify the meal into four groups, with a range within each group reflecting the selectivity of the dragon for the meal.

Group A – from A_1 (tenderloin only)
                to A_5 (choice and second cuts, including some skeletal tissue)

Group B – from B₁   (most of the readily available flesh without skeletal
and connective tissue)

to B₄   (all available flesh with some skeletal and
connective tissue)

Group C – from C₁   (all possible flesh)

to C₂   (all flesh and up to 25 percent of all skeletal and
connective tissue and/or hide).

Except in one instance, these three categories accounted for all kills in the first thirty-seven months of the study. The exception was a dragon who had not been seen previously, and who then returned to a normal feeding pattern. Al-Jerez speculates that this animal was newly awakened from either a long sleep or a hoarding period (DNDI:SIP 5, 11).

Group D – from D₁   (all readily available meat and up to 50 percent of
nonmeat portions of the trunk, excluding all
extremities)

to D₄   (all flesh, at least 75 percent of nonmeat tissue, the
head, and up to four of the five extremities)

Kills in the D₅ category had to be deduced by subtracting the number of the remaining cattle from the pre-raid count. Seventy-six cattle fell into the D₅ group (DNDI:SIP 13). Plate XV demonstrates the findings of the Interface Study. All D kills but one were made during the final three months: an impressive picture of the voraciousness of the Frenzy appetite.

Here are two representative entries in the log of feeding raids at the Wad Madani site (DNDI:SIP 4).

June 23: Dragon Four – A₄ kill, time: 28 minutes. Stoop Pattern.

4:23 p.m. Dragon Four airborne at 65 meters approaching from southwest over 416. Circles twice, slowing. Herd unaware and quiet. Sky overcast, no shadow. Wind 7 knots from NE. Four stoops at 4:26, strikes #84679J at back of neck, one blow with left foreleg, kills. Herd runs to trees. Four removes skin from exposed surface, eats meat from shoulder, flank, and rump. Rolls carcass to expose other side, skins main trunk, eats shoulder, flank, and rump. No skeletal or connective tissue taken. Large conglomerations of fat removed. Skinning time, 20 seconds, side one; 32 seconds, side two. Feeding time: 7 min., 23 sec. side one; 9 min., 14 sec. side two. Airborne 4:53 p.m., flies directly SW.

July 16: Dragon Two – B₄ kill, time: 5 minutes+. Stealth Pattern.

Two appears as he strikes #84665J on left rear, 6:12 a.m. No alarm from herd before strike. No sign of Two before strike. ?Mime assumed before dawn, in position along path to water tank. Removes head, takes forequarters and rump, including skeletal and connective tissue. Total feeding time: 3 min., 42 sec. Airborne 6:16 a.m., flies WSW.

XV. Ingestive Preference at Wad Madani

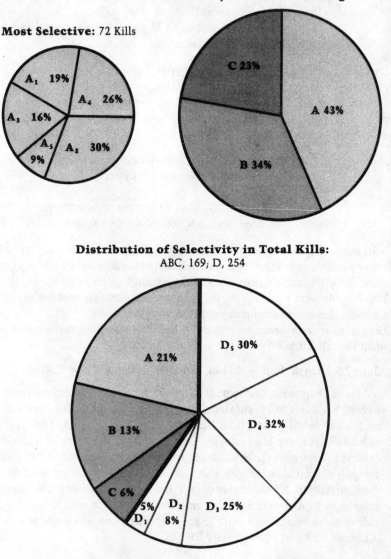

Most Selective: 72 Kills

A₁ 19%
A₄ 26%
A₃ 16%
A₅ 9%
A₂ 30%

Selectivity in Normal Feeding: 169 Kills

C 23%
A 43%
B 34%

Distribution of Selectivity in Total Kills:
ABC, 169; D, 254

A 21%
D₅ 30%
D₄ 32%
B 13%
D₃ 25%
C 6%
5% D₂ 8%
D₁

This chart was prepared by Mustafa al-Jerez for the Dragon, Non-Dragon Interface Project Study in Ingestive Preference.

A second test site, similar to that at Wad Madani, was established on the grazing lands above the Jabal Al-Awliyā Dam, four months after the Wad Madani project was under way. Once the cattle were in place, dragon foragers appeared without coaxing. There was some duplication of hunters at both sites. The purpose of the Jabal Al-Awliyā site is to test methods of protecting cattle and other stock from feeding raids. A variety of methods have been installed with mixed results: vocal persuasion, laser shielding, odor deployment, and the Boumani Sonic Net, which was developed on the site. The results of the experiments performed at this site are published in *The Dragon, Non-Dragon Interface: Techniques of Deterrent and Defense*.

The least effective means employed to date has been vocal persuasion. The research team assembled recordings in the percussive language and in actual speech, requesting that cattle not be taken. In fifteen possible raids there were fifteen failures of this system for a total of twenty-three cattle (DNDI:TDD 2). The most successful defense system has proved to be the old-fashioned barn. Cattle kept in an open shed were almost as vulnerable as cattle in the open field: fourteen raids attempted, thirteen completed for a loss of twenty head. However, the cattle kept completely under cover have not been attacked since the beginning of the project except for one instance. For the barn to be an effective installation for raising beef cattle on a large scale, important problems of engineering and architecture remain in designing a structure that can be built economically to house several hundred head at once under hygienic conditions (DNDI:TDD 18).

Even the barn is not proof against all attack, however. Dragons #7 and #8 from the Wad Madani site on a Feeding Frenzy strike drove the animals out of the barn. Dragon #7 removed the double doors from the southwest entrance to the barn, and the frightened cattle huddled in the fenced lot where they were conveniently confined for the dragons to feed. Two nights later after the doors had been replaced, #7 again removed the doors and the loading ramp, while #8 set fire to the northeast wall of the barn, before rejoining his mate in the lot. The cattle ran from the fire into the jaws of the dragons. A total loss of 654 head. Clearly the barn system will not protect cattle from dragons in the Feeding Frenzy (DNDI:TDD 38).

Three other methods have been tested against dragon raids in the open. The first to be installed was the laser shield. The cattle are confined to a one-acre field. The perimeters of the field are set with a series of electric eyes aimed six meters above the ground. When an object passes through the beams of the electric eyes, a grid of laser beams is activated, shining just above the backs of the cattle. The system is an elaboration of the flash photography harassment that was at least partly effective at Lake Hawea. It deters dragon raids about 40 percent of the time. However, unless the system of lasers is operated manually, the network reacts to any object, even bats or small birds or windborne detritus, as readily as it does to dragons, so that the cattle are constantly harassed by the beams, and do not prosper (DNDI:TDD 20).

The Interface Defense group developed the Boumani Sonic Net, which emits a high-pitched, metallic shriek almost inaudible to the human ear. It, too, is effective about 40 percent of the time and has gained some acceptance in the beef industry because it is more cheaply installed than the laser shield and can be repaired more easily. However, weight-gain in cattle raised under the net does not approach that of cattle raised in the open (DNDI:TDD 31). Recently noxious odors have been tested with some success against dragons circling in the initial phase of the Stoop Pattern. The system must be operated manually, requiring a twenty-four-hour guard and is effective only 23 percent of the time. In addition, the cattle do not react favorably to the odor of decaying flesh, which is by far the most effective odor tested so far (DNDI:TDD 39).

There is one consideration of overriding importance: once a dragon has committed himself to taking his prey, he will not yield (DNDI:TDD 10). A dragon in the Feeding Frenzy can never be deterred even in the initial phase of his run, except by direct, life-threatening attack. He will defend himself thoroughly against any interference, destroying his attacker before returning to his kill. And he will take revenge. The entire Jabal Al-Awliyā herd had to be replaced after the research team attempted to use antiaircraft and tank weapons against a frenzied pair (DNDI: TDD 42).

Since the Interface study has shown that 60 percent of the cattle killed at Wad Madani, and a like proportion at Jabal Al-Awliyā, were slaughtered by dragons in the Feeding Frenzy, the usefulness of any defense system currently under study is seriously in question; especially when the effectiveness of the system is weighed against the enormous expense of the installation and the adverse effect the defense systems have on the cattle themselves. The Japanese have installed an elaborate and costly system to protect the Nagata Museum and other national treasures. Expense of installation was not a consideration. Taking advantage of the radio-interference pattern laid down by rapidly moving dragons, they have constructed a grid of monitors throughout the main islands. By watching this grid, they can track the movements of all dragons within their territory. The Museum and other sites are effectively defended by hypersonics (Yamaguchi, *Kokuhō no Hogo*). It is possible that some derivative of this system can be developed for agricultural use. The system has not been tested against a dragon in the throes of Hoard Lust, however, so it is not necessarily fully dependable against Feeding Frenzy.

Marsden, who was consulted in the initial phases of the Interface study, speculated on the dragon menace, suggesting that while it was on an international scale an interesting fact, it did not become an alarming fact except in specific localities at specific times. Even at the height of the pre-mating period the total number of livestock taken by dragons is not large when compared to the world supply. Given more efficient husbandry, we should be able to maintain both our population and theirs, providing they do not continue to multiply geometrically for an indefinite time. The global problem, as he saw it, is to be sure that those areas that do come under the scourge of dragon feeding do not suffer unnecessarily. Any area being vulnerable, all areas should be interested in the survival of the one victimized. In the long run the most effective defense against the depletion of red meat supplies by dragon raids may turn out to be the institution of more

XVI. South Island, New Zealand. The upper reaches of the Rakaia River were claimed by dragons as they were establishing their hegemony over Stewart Island. This and various other scenic areas of the South Island are now too dangerous for agricultural activities of any kind. Low impact visits by fluent Dragon speakers are tolerated. (*Photo: L. MacDonald*)

efficient meat production methods. He suggested that the resources of the Sudanese project be turned to this problem, where a quick solution was more likely. His project recommendation report ends: 'Dragons evidently consider it their right to have the unimpeded freedom to eat when, what, where, and how much they please. For them the natural order is arranged in a strict hierarchy with dragons firmly at the top. At the moment and for the foreseeable future we simply do not have the knowledge or techniques to challenge this assumption' (DNDI: TDD 1).

Language

Dragons communicate by gesture, percussion, bellow, and voice. They have a complex system of percussive signals produced by thumping the ground with their tails or striking resonant material with their front or hind feet. Given their size and power, they have a wide choice of material for resonance: hard-packed sand, small caverns, or water serve their purposes as well as the more conventional wood or metal. They can rattle the spiny protrusions along the backbone, which produces a clicking sound. By shaking their tails in midflight, they can make a melodious soft clanging, which is apparently a form of affectionate address. In groups of two or three they converse by sighs, stamping, snorts, and steam. They have the usual range of body signals, augmented by a full six appendages and a long tail as well as the collar and the spiny ridge. Combinations of all these possibilities form the percussive language, the communication of day-to-day living among dragons (Marsden, Lex, 4–10).

The distinctive dragon bellow vibrates with the hollow roar associated with big cats, though the sound can be much louder on occasion and is usually more bass. It can be a mere thrumming, a kind of modified purr, or, as a warning or threat, it can be literally earthshaking. Before the fact of dragon presence was widely accepted, the bellow was identified as jet noise or thunder (viz. USADC Bul 7356jk/se998:5). Contented dragons, especially in the company of other dragons underground, bellow simultaneously, working the vibration into a long, repetitive song, with intricate rhythmic variations and subtle harmonies. They take great pleasure in this group creation and become enraged if interrupted. This form of communication is discussed more fully below under 'Wandering: The Arts'.

The bellow, like a puppy's growl, comes with practice and age, as the empty chambers develop. Kits must be taught the discipline of percussive and bellow communication. The boisterous exploitation of these sounds can incite the parents to anger, though this is the only known occasion on which dragons can be anticipated to lose their tempers with their young. If the roil becomes too rambunctious in their thumping, shaking, bellowing, and snorting, the attendant parent will quiet them with a full bellow (Froedlich, ABD, 15).

In addition to the percussive language and bellow, all dragons have actual speech, as was assumed during the Pre-Medieval Infestation, according to the New Zealand verminologists. The voice is not produced in the hollow chambers of the neck and head, which form the bellow and give it the distinctive resonance. Speech sounds are produced by air blowing across vocal cords whose tautness can be regulated at will, as is true of human speech (Froedlich, ABD, 247). The dragon can disguise his voice as cleverly as he can mime, and throw it as a ventriloquist does, so that it is impossible to distinguish it from naturally occurring sounds or from the cries of other creatures. However, if a dragon chooses to speak with a non-dragon, he uses a direct, conversational tone that can be accepted as his 'natural' voice. The voice is clear throughout several octaves and does not blur either in whispering or shouting. The sound is curiously pleasing. It carries a distinct vibration that cannot be heard but is detected in the sinuses. Those who have had actual conversations with dragons report an after-effect – a curious light-headedness, close to euphoria (St. James, NZSDSWP 4).

Dragon language is precise and elegant, with an immense store of words. St. James describes the vocabulary as 'geologic', with sounds classified as water, wind, fire, and earth related, including a range of metallic noises. Sounds from one geologic group can be combined into complete sentences, or sounds from the full geologic range are mixed. The ongoing study of dragon language is centered at the New Zealand School of Dragon Studies, and information is published in their journal as the results become available (St. James, NZSDSWP 4).

In the single record of a dragon hatch (that is, birth) the young appeared to speak immediately, and the parents employed their full vocabularies from the outset. Thus it is not clear whether the young acquire vocabularies through exposure to parental speech or if the language is in fact innate, though this latter seems doubtful (Grenner and Del Rio, RevZoo 4:7:6).

Dragons are curious about human languages and can be bribed with words they have not heard before. Though they are quick to spot a fraud, they can be enticed in this manner as they never can with gold or precious stones (DNDI:TDD 1). They appear to be able to reconstruct whole languages from a few sentences, and are enormously scornful of human limitations on this matter. For the most part, they will speak only in their own tongue, leaving it up to the listener to translate as best he can. Few humans can be said to have mastered this language. Marsden came closest to being fluent. Froedlich, Santander, and Branco were able to make themselves understood. Among the second generation of verminologists, Grenner and Del Rio made a hopeful beginning; Philomel St. James and Sean Jones from the New Zealand School are the most proficient. They have seven students in the initial stages of learning. St. James comes closest to Marsden in mastering the language. She has used it actively for almost thirty years and considers herself about 20 percent proficient.

Besides actually understanding and being understood, a further difficulty in conversing with a dragon, even if he condescends to use human vocabulary, is that his memory is measured in hundreds, rather than in tens of years, and his perspective is relentlessly dragon.[1]

Although they are possibly sufficiently intelligent to master the skill and probably have the anatomical capability, it is doubtful that dragons read. With one exception, they have shown no interest in books. Though books are often unearthed in dragon hoards, they are usually elaborately made books, collected probably for the binding or illustration, or because they were greatly prized by

---

[1] This brief description of dragon language follows the outline established by the New Zealand School of Dragon Studies on the subject. It is the suspicion of the verminological community at large that the 'complexity' of dragon language may very well be the result of its being not a true language at all, but merely a collection of voluntarily produced though meaningless sounds, some of which reappear in short patterns. The human mind will seek to impose an orderly form on any random pattern, and will strive for meaning even in chaos. They believe that it is this human characteristic that has created 'Dragon'. If this hypothesis is indeed correct, dragon language can be said to exist exactly as cloud castles exist – as perceived, rather than independent phenomena. [See A. McArdle. 'A Reinterpretation', ZR 28:2:18–21].

the victims of the hoarding raid. Thus, when the people of Rafaela sent their delegation to beg the exchange of *La Biblia Sumamenta Santa* in return for the spring lambs of the three succeeding years, they only insured that the dingy volume would be placed at the bottom of the hoard instead of being cast out on the trash heap beside the entrance to the lair where Alejandro had found *Le Libro de los Laberintos* (Lucan, *The Destruction of San Cristóbal*, 154).

It is certain that dragons do not write. No evidence of any kind of dragon inscription has ever been found, not even any patterned scratching or marring in the earth. Given their unerringly precise memories, perhaps writing or even reading has no particular usefulness to them (Marsden, NZSDSWP 9). Their aesthetic sense is satisfied in Knots and Chants. (See 'Wandering: the Arts' below). Bruford's expeditions in search of the reputed 'dragon book of all time' were exercises in futility, and the recent attempts to revive them are ill-advised. (This project is being funded by an international media organization through the University of Penfirth. The funds could be better used in a more fruitful area of study).

The one dragon who has shown any curiosity about books is Vlad. According to Marsden's private papers, this dragon asked him to read aloud from Shakespeare. He particularly enjoyed portions from the Henriad. Marsden also read to him from other books, apparently. Vlad asked him to stop reading the *Iliad* because he had to read it in translation. They tried a variety of twentieth-century authors: Lawrence, Faulkner, Conrad. Vlad particularly liked Garcia-Marquez's *Cien Años de Soledad*, though he corrected Marsden's pronunciation of the Spanish constantly, insisting on a Colombian accent from the Piedmont. After two paragraphs of *Le Voyeur*, Vlad impaled it on a claw and incinerated it. This dragon apparently had a particular interest in human beings and their culture, and his curiosity is clearly anomalous.

Even histories of dragons, which might be thought to appeal to their vanity, refer to events that they remember independently, and do not arouse their interest. The remaking of past time through its relation in 'history' is, in effect, a human study of human capacity, and irrelevant to dragons. The only human crafts that interest them are smithying, as might be expected, riddling and rhyming, and animal husbandry. An occasional dragon will listen to poetry with some signs of patience or even enjoyment (Marsden, NZSDSWP 6).

Wandering: Observation

Except for times spent in hoarding or in raising young, the adult life of the dragon is spent in what dragons term 'Wandering'. As the name implies, the dragon has no fixed abode, but travels from place to place according to his inclination. He is almost always alone (Marsden, NZSDSWP 11). Occasionally he will travel to an established meeting ground to spend time in company of other dragons. Stewart Island is such a gathering place, as are, to a lesser extent, the Faeroe Islands, and Paramushir and the northernmost of the Kurile Islands. Hunting is

XVII. Kaikoura, South Island, New Zealand. These former seal beaches provide a near-perfect dragon environment: cool, temperate climate with dramatic scenery; easy access to abundant natural and domesticated food stocks; straightforward defensibility; proximity to a permanent colony – Stewart Island.
(*Photo: L. MacDonald*)

easy for him and doesn't occupy much time. Most of his time during the Wandering is spent in Observation.

Observation, as such, is an activity peculiar to dragons. When he is engaged in Observation, a dragon will spend days or even weeks in the same spot, shifting to catch the sun, but mostly motionless, eyes open, watching what appears to be a static scene. The dragon prefers elevated positions with a wide, unobstructed view, preferably within easy distance of a reliable marine or terrestrial food supply. A dragon may return to the same spot repeatedly. During Observation the dragon, though motionless, is always alert. He appears to divide his attention into two phases. In one phase his attention is directed outward. During the outward phase of his Observation the dragon is apparently watching, even perhaps recording, the details of the natural scene around him. An ingenious study by Ure McAlister of the University of Auckland attempted to discover if there was any relationship between known Observation sites and zones of recent orogeny. The results were inconclusive, however, since roughly half the sites were in areas

XVIII. Miles of uninhabited beaches in Southern Chile are strewn with half-mimed
dragons in Observation. Undisturbed, they remain immobile for
weeks at a time. (*Photo: L. MacDonald*)

where no dramatic geologic activity was present (McAlister, U. of Auckland,
Ph.D. diss.).

In the second phase, although the dragon will startle immediately at any
untoward movement or sound, his attention appears to be focused with great
intensity inside himself: the eyes glaze and the pupils enlarge and contract without
reference to exterior illumination. This inward phase is apparently given to
remembering or reconstructing past events. Occasionally he may show signs of
anger or amusement, steaming or stamping suddenly in response to no apparent
impetus (DNDI:SIP 16). He shifts from one phase to the other randomly,
regardless of the time of day or the duration of each phase. All our information
about the dragon's perception of the purpose of his Observation comes from the
conversation between Marsden and Vlad, which concludes the present work.

When the first sightings of dragons in Observation were made, verminologists
struggled to get as much information as possible in a short time, relying on
hand-operated cameras and round-the clock monitoring (Steinmetz, 59th ICA
Proceedings). A more efficient technique for recording such data has been

developed by Visplex Associates, working with the research group at the University of Khartoum. A series of at least three cameras with telephoto lenses and stop-motion capabilities is placed in shielded positions with at least one camera focused on the scene that the dragon is observing. If the cameras are positioned without alerting the beast, they can be left to run automatically, recording one frame at appropriate intervals (of fifteen minutes, for example) without the loss of information of any significance. By checking on the subject once a day, the study team may record an entire observation but remain free to pursue other work (DNDI:SIP 16).

If the dragon is at an Observation site, he may go into an elaborate mime, rather than move. A remarkable record of this process was made by accident five years ago by a Princeton team on a sighting expedition on the Cascades of western North America. They dismantled their cameras when a routine check showed that the specimen they had been recording for two weeks had left the site, and nothing remained in the spot but coarse gravel and twigs with a few strands of grass. Severe thunderstorms and subsequent flooding prevented them from retrieving a third camera, which they had lodged in a sheltered crevice that could be approached only by a long climb. When they returned three days later, they were startled to see that the dragon was still there. When the camera was finally recovered, the film proved to be a record of the dragon in the process of assuming his disguise, the mime period, and the gradual fading of the mime during the course of the thunderstorm. During the period of mimic disguise a team of four rock climbers had maneuvered their way up the cliff face and rested on a small shelf, oblivious of the dragon only meters away (Troutt, *Princeton Review*, 3:42).

Wandering: Recreation

The sea provides their true recreation. Dragons love water and spend long years asleep (and perhaps in Observation) on the ocean floor or floating in the submarine currents. Their presence warms the sea around them, causing abnormalities in the size of indigenous populations of sea creatures and vegetation. They swim as easily as they fly, folding their limbs and wings tightly against their bodies and lashing their tails. If they choose they can dive to great depths to elude detection or to pursue prey (Jones, NZSDSWP 15). Dragons will fly great distances to drink and swim in the seawater they crave, alighting on the surface in billows of steam, riding the waves comfortably, drinking water, or waiting for prey. Young or playful dragons skim over the surface of the sea, scooping water with their open jaws into long foam-crested wakes, or boiling it with fountains of flame. They appear to enjoy playing with dolphins and porpoises, mimicking their rolling motion (Marsden and Jones, NZSDSWP 9). This is the only known instance of dragons habitually seeking and enjoying the companionship of other creatures. (They are often accompanied by bats, of course. These mammals share their habit of night flight and their caves, but dragons seem not to notice them).

Dragons can fly from the ocean surface, rising by the power of their wings, but

XIX. The Brooks Range of Alaska is a favorite Observation area.
Note the trio in the sunshine at the middle right.
(*Photo: George B. Wharton, Jr*)

XX. Remote, scenic areas, like the North Crater of volcanic Mount Wrangell, Alaska, are exactly suited for dragon recreation. (*Photo: George B. Wharton, Jr*)

this is a slow and awkward process, similar to the ungainly takeoff of the gooney bird of the Galápagos Islands. If the depth allows, they prefer to become airborne by catapulting themselves from the ocean floor. This allows them to explode from the surface of the sea in a spout of steam and smoke, going directly from sea to full flight (Jones, DSGDP, No. 47). The process of diving and leaping from the sea is part of the mating display, the pair competing for speed, noise, and fountain, or cooperating in creating voluminous columns of water and steam (St. James, NZSDSWP 7).

Dragons like cold temperatures. Altitude does not appear to be a factor, so they can enjoy the glaciers of the highest mountains. The rugged terrain of the alps of the world provides an ideal combination of frigid temperatures and seclusion. Even the Fourth Census, with all its sophisticated technology, probably missed a significant number of dragons in the folds of the Himalayas and the Andes.

On calm winter days at sea in the extreme latitudes, dragons lie on the pack ice or swim under it, melting their way upward. The crew of the Canadian freighter *Little France*, stranded in the ice of Lake Superior one night in December, watched in superstitious horror as the red glow of a dragon body rose slowly through the ice at their prow. The dragon crawled onto the ice, still burning, and slid slowly northeast, leaving a straight track of open water in his wake. (See 'Freighter Crew Rescued by Dragon', *Sudbury Herald*, CVII:43:12:3).

The fury of severe storms seems to excite them. Men on the drilling rigs in the North and Beaufort seas have watched congregations of dragons playing during storms. Their bodies become incandescent and show fitfully through the snow, and their bellowing sounds above the wind. As the storm abates, the dragons disappear, leaving strangely shaped ice forms as the only evidence of their play (*Canadian Photographer*, 3:45–50).

Apparently they also amuse themselves by watching human activities. According to studies by Marsden and St. James, dragons situate themselves at will even in the heart of large metropolitan centers and remain for many days in mime, watching the passing scene (NZSDSWP 9). From time to time a dragon will be spotted in the air over an urban area. Young dragons have been known to come to cities, as if to an amusement park, perching on buildings or garlanding themselves on pedestrian overpasses. The highway complex in Westchester County, New York, known as Hawthorne Circle, was visited by four young dragons who wound themselves along the bridges and around the pylons, disrupting traffic in the noon hour (*The New York Times*). Every few years a dragon or dragon pair will stop off at Ontario Place in Toronto after a hunting expedition to the west around Kitchener. They like to lie along the bridges crossing from Toronto to the islands and watch the boat traffic passing underneath (*Toronto Globe and Mail*).[2]

Wandering: The Arts, Knotting, and the Chant

Dragons themselves do not create what could properly be called Arts. They do not seek to improve their surroundings or to manifest an aesthetic drive in a permanent way as humans do. The homely arts that embellish the elements of survival in the human community – architecture, painting, photography, and so forth – do not have dragon counterparts. Though they hoard the so-called minor arts of human civilization and add sculptures in precious metals and stone to their piles, they do not experiment with creating out of materials themselves. Their

---

[2] The author was privileged to watch a dragon at play in the Falls of the Niagara River in the late afternoon on a snowy day. Very few people were visiting the Falls that day. I was looking over the guardrail at the Canadian Falls and was startled to see a large green dragon swoop down out of the heavy sky. He flew through the flume over and over again, and swam in the icy river at the lip of the Falls. He did not challenge the force of the water as it plunged over the precipice, nor did he venture into the Cauldron. After ten minutes of this sport he flew to the top of the Skylon Tower, and crawled down onto the top of the elevator inching its way up the outside. The Skylon personnel managed to evacuate the seven passengers from the elevator as soon as it reached the top, and they let the elevator run back down, hoping to drive off the dragon. He remained coiled up on the roof of the elevator for another two round trips before he flew off down river through the snow.

XXI. Belgrade Lakes, Maine, USA. For years a mated pair have commandeered this rocky point of land, engaging in what are apparently vocalization contests with the migratory loon population. Although these reverberatory displays have disrupted the local summer economy, loon counts on this and adjacent lakes have soared.
(*Photo: Philomel St. James*)

only artistic outlets, if we may call them that, are the Knot and the Chant, which are group efforts and exist only in the moment of their performance.

The Knot is a 'celebration of time and three-dimensional space', according to Philomel St. James. The dragons themselves are the Knot, twining around each other or arranging themselves without touching in relationship to each other. On the ground the Knot can be a compact ball of dragons or spread out over many square meters. In the air they exploit the freedom of altitude and range. As it progresses, the Knot moves freely from ground to air and back, through a complex series of interrelated forms. Presumably they perform knotting in the ocean as well, though this has not been observed. The Knot may be performed by as few as two dragons or by a whole colony. It has symmetry at each stage of the performance, and the whole performance has a pattern. Working with Masaji Tsuruta, St. James has filmed eight Knots over a period of twelve years, and has analyzed them to show their relationship to classical dance choreography, to architectural use of space, and to traditional music forms. A publication of this work, including four tapes of Knots, is in preparation (St. James, NZSDSWP 23).

As the Knot is an expression of space and duration, the Chant is an exploration of duration and sound: dragon music. Dragons do not Chant alone, only in company, the relationship between the participants being an integral part of the Chant. The Chants themselves are quite varied: mournful, cheerful, puckish, brief, extended, concentrated, or long and exploratory, even mechanical and monotonous. They can be created entirely in the resonating chambers, or with the voice alone, or in combination – *a cappella*, or accompanied by the full range of percussive sound. Dragons make no effort to repeat Chants, even those made by the same group. Nor can a dragon's attention be held by recordings of his previous Chants, nor the Chants of other groups (DNDI:TDD 4).

Studies of the Chant record 434 examples collected over a period of 63 years, on 14 separate sites. Some of these examples (23) are single Chants by casual groups. The largest single collection (207) was made by Marsden during his stay on Ascension. The remainder were collected in small batches in various locations. No Chant among this entire repertoire repeats any other except in the most general ways, such as attention to rhythmic pattern and variation on motif. The Chants may be grouped geographically, or by participants, by developmental stage of individual dragons, or by climate, season, time of day, or by interval since feeding, but no pattern can be constructed by which another Chant can be predicted as to mood, tone, rhythm, or range (B. Hansen, MIT, Ph.D. diss. This esoteric literature has not been studied by musicologists but might yield to the sophisticated analysis appropriate to music).

The most widely known Chant, the 'Ta-Toc', was recorded by Marsden on Ascension. It was the spontaneous creation of eight young dragons as they emerged from their sleeping cave into a thick fog. The popular Vapex recording is the complete Chant: eight minutes. Marsden gives the following account of the making of that recording, and a clue to dragon attitude toward the Chant.

4:35 a.m., near dawn, May 22: I was repairing the recorder to complete the bird calls for the University of London which had to be sent off that afternoon when the Foundation sent the supply plane to the island. I had been up through the night rewiring the microphone and had only got it working when the first kit, Demon, emerged from the Sleeping Cave at Round Point. The parents were not in the area, the female having left long before and Thamock off on a sea hunt. Demon was huffing softly as he climbed to the entrance. I could hear his claws clicking on the tunnel floor, and was testing the microphone by trying to record these faint sounds at 225 meters.

It was cool for May and raining finely. As he emerged I could barely identify him through the mist and fog except aurally. The shape of his head is distinctive, with its curious fore-knob, but the 'huff-huffle, huff-huffle' was absolute identification. He stretched his wings and tail with evident pleasure and let out the long, sibilant breath which I have learned to associate with 'come and see this'. The remaining seven kits joined him quickly. (Technically they were nearly sexually mature and therefore should be called stern and stiera, of course, but they still were kits to me). They flew short bursts, more leaping than flying, and became more excited and pleased, glowing faintly through the gray of pre-dawn. Greta, who was inverted over the heads of her siblings, began a low crooning rumble of pleasure. [This is the first sound of the Vapex recording. The preliminary 12 meters of tape record steaming and shuffling and have been eliminated by the company for commercial reasons]. All of a sudden, in concert, the whole roil burst into the complicated Chant. It lasted eight minutes. The small stern whom I called Barf beat a drone on the spongy forest floor with his tail. The experience of standing in the mist, 100 meters from the nearest dragon, on the quivering earth, surrounded by the resonance of this Chant, is beyond description. They were enormously pleased with themselves afterward, brushing by one another, snorting and steaming, and beating the ground with their rear feet in the sure signs of dragon hilarity. Though they quieted down at sunrise, they remained cheerful and self-satisfied throughout the day, occasionally steaming at one another, or stamping suddenly.

Hoarding

A dragon intent on hoarding is utterly single-minded and therefore more dangerous than he is at any other time. In the Feeding Frenzy dragons are enormously destructive, especially in pairs, but they retain the normal instinct to survive and can be turned aside by sufficient threat or by sufficient inconvenience. It is the latter that forms the basis for all defense systems (DNDI:TDD 10). A dragon in the throes of hoarding, however, is overcome by lust and will pursue treasure in the face of seemingly certain destruction. His powers of cunning, guile, and sheer violence are at their height. Here is an account from the Mexico edition of the *International Herald Tribune* of the destruction of the Archaeological Museum of Mexico. It is a good example of the resourceful determination of a dragon subdued by Hoard lust.

MUSEU ARCEOLOGICA FALLS IN DRAGON RAID
(MÉXICO DF. AP) The world-famous archaeological museum of México DF was destroyed by a dragon last evening. Authorities estimate that one-third of the world's most valuable collection of antique gold was carried off by the beast. Police and army personnel were unable to stop the dragon, nicknamed 'Cortez', from collecting pre-Colombian gold and precious stones stored in the award-winning museum. The remains of the museum are under twenty-four-hour guard.
    The dragon dropped into the center courtyard at 2:23 a.m. and killed watchmen on duty, according to the sole survivor, Ramon Escheva, who

managed to escape through a narrow side door and sound the alarm. Before the police could respond, the dragon had moved quickly from room to room, breaking display cases. By the time the police arrived, the dragon had piled her choices in the courtyard and was beginning to fly off with them, carrying the best pre-Colombian gold in Mexico in her feet and jaws. As she cleared the roof she paused to destroy the central pillar with her tail. Police captain Jorge Santos reports that during this maneuver the dragon dropped a large gold mask. Despite gunfire and grenades, she re-entered the crumbling museum to retrieve her prize. Police and army stood helplessly by, watching as the dragon flew off toward Pueblo. Fighter planes from the Mexican and US Air Force were called out to pursue her, but were unsuccessful in locating the dragon. Her present location has not been determined.

Sr. Geraldo Serreno, director of the museum, speculated this morning that the dragon had probably been on the roof of the Museo for several days. Guards had reported an unusual warmth on Thursday, and the Fire Department had been called in to investigate. Dra. Consuela Beniquez from the Zoological Gardens in Chapultepec identified the dragon from photographs taken by the security cameras at the Museo as the same female who had raided the museum at Colima last month. Sr. Serreno reports that an estimate of the damage will be prepared after the site has been cleaned up and an assessment of the loss to the collection can be made. There are no plans to reconstruct the Museo at the moment, but Sr. Serreno stated, 'Eventually the precious heritage of the past will again be properly housed in the heart of Mexico's greatest city'.

The hoard is secreted away in a remote spot, typically a high mountain cave or crevice. The dragon makes repeated forays to increase his pile. Once he has amassed his treasure and arranged it to his liking, he guards it with his very life. He seldom tolerates any intrusions by any being except bats. He emerges infrequently and briefly to feed, keeping within sight of his lair. He sits on his hoard a long time. It is quite possible that Cortez, who amassed her hoard thirteen years ago, will be with it into the next century and beyond. Harada speculated that 150 years is about the minimum time (Harada, NFR 9).

We know that dragons hoard, we know that very few dragons are hoarding at any one time, and we know that their piles are usually deposits of great wealth, although idiosyncratic piles have been discovered. We do not know why dragons hoard. Why should a beast of such power, a beast virtually untouched by time, disease, or famine, have such an overweening lust for something that is utterly useless to him?

Dragons do have a definite appreciation for what we would call beauty, both on a grand scale – their observation and resting places are uniformly situated to provide scenic exposure as well as comfort and seclusion – and in miniature. Grenner and Del Rio watched a dragon picking his way across an open field, carefully avoiding patches of violets and forget-me-nots in bloom (Grenner and

XXII. Contents of Known Hoards

Item	Taibaishan	Kirensk	Nagata	Vlad*
Gold, raw	XXX			
wrought, 0–3oz		XXX	000	000
wrought, 3oz +		000	XXX	000
Silver, raw	XXX			
wrought, 0–3oz			000	000
wrought, 3oz +			000	0
Other wrought metal				
small pieces		0	0	000
large pieces		0	0	000
Gems, uncut	XXX	0	0	000
cut, or in settings		XXX	XXX	000
Semiprecious stones uncut	000	000	000	0
cut, or in settings		XXX	XXX	000
Ceramics		0	000	XXX
Mixed materials		0	0	000
Sculpture		0	000	000
Technological bric-a-brac				000
Other				
Shells (Tristan da Cunha only)				
Plastics				0
Bones				XXX

0	Occasional pieces
000	Well-represented in the collection
XXX	Major interest of the collector

*uncatalogued

Chart from *Nagata Reports*, 94.
Used by permission.

Del Rio, ZooJ IX:45). The contents of hoards are not uniformly beautiful, however, and do not seem to have been selected with an aesthetic criterion, so a greedy lust to have quantities of beautiful objects is not a likely motivation for hoarding.

The hoard found on Tristan da Cunha was a complete collection of every type of nautilus and conch shell found in the South Atlantic. The hoard at Revelstoke consisted principally of plastic items. There has been a suggestion that it was a practice hoard, gathered by a young dragon, though this is merely speculation. These are the two hoards on record that did not include any of the treasure usually associated with dragons. As a gesture of trust, Vlad allowed St. James to see his pile. She was not prepared for the size and splendor of the hoard. In addition to the standard gold, it contained some idiosyncratic items, notably an enormous collection of primate skulls. (St. James was not allowed to handle or photograph them and was not taken to the lair again. When she returned to the island with new equipment for photographing them and dating, the island was deserted and the lair had been emptied).

The hoard uncovered near Kirensk in the Central Siberian Uplands was entirely made up of uncut gems and raw gold, as if the dragon had grubbed them from the earth, dumped them helter-skelter into his lair, and lain on them for two hundred years (Harada, NR 23). By contrast, the Worm of Nagata had sorted through the pile he gathered, discarding some items, which Hashima and his party found strewn about the valley in varying stages of decomposition. His lair was carefully arranged with the wrought gold, jade, and gems in the center, forming the bed. Silver and lesser stones lined the walls. A service for twelve of Rogers Brothers '1812' silver plate was found scattered about the entrance outside. This dragon did not collect wood carving, textiles, or paintings, though he apparently had had the treasures of half the world to choose from.

The hoard at Taibaishan apparently had been collected several hundred years ago. Although this pile was in the western mountains of China, no dragon levy coins were included. A thick deposit of soil covered the pile, and generations of creatures had lived over it. When it was first discovered, it was thought to be a grave site, until anthropologists denied that any human burial could be arranged as this pile was, and no human skeletal remains were found (Hayashiya, NR 83).

At present there are at least three dragons sitting on piles: a dragon in the mountains of the Northern Korean Peninsula, the dragon who destroyed San Cristóbal, and Cortez. These three beasts have collected gold and gems – conforming exactly to type.

Speculation about dragon psychology is a risky undertaking. However, the verminologists at the University of Kyōto have studied the hoarding phenomenon exhaustively, and their analysis of the contents of known dragon hoards has suggested a possible motivation to them that is at least partially substantiated by the testimony of Vlad. (The conversation with Marsden containing this insight appears at the end of Part III).

They have suggested two criteria for the selection of booty: first, the dragon's own taste, which guides a compulsive collecting drive; second and more impor-

XXIII. The entrance to Vlad's hoard on The Snares, New Zealand. Philomel St.
James took this photograph at the mouth of the lair after she found the
island deserted and the hoard empty. (*Photo: NZSDS*)

tant, the immutability of the object collected. In no pile have they discovered
items or the remains of items that break down significantly with the passage of
time. Dr Shigehara and his team propose that individual dragons are stricken by
the idea of mortality and gather valuable items that please them and that do not
change as time goes by. The hoard is the dragon's assurance that everything will
not fade and turn to dust. Eventually the lust for the hoard lessens and the dragon
loses interest and returns to the Wandering (Shigehara, NFR 20. The Revelstoke
hoard was hardly 'valuable' by human standards, of course, but this assessment
of the market value of one hoard would not, in itself, disprove Professor
Shigehara's theory).

Mating

We do not know as yet why any one dragon ends the Wandering period in either
procreation or in hoarding. Nor do we know how dragons choose their mates,
though we do know that a pair will remain mated for more than one roil. Some

XXIV. A dragon enthusiast explores ice shapes formed during the mating display
at Crested Butte, Colorado. (*Photo: ULA Wirephoto*)

courtship displays have been noted recently, and there are scattered reports of pairs in flight, but the hard information on mating is still quite scarce.

Preparation for mating entails the Feeding Frenzy described above. Apparently the choice of mate is made during the feeding cycle, the pair traveling long distances to find each other. The feeding continues after they have located each other, the two courting dragons then sharing plunder – a situation that is particularly dangerous, as the raids at Wad Madani demonstrate. Once the mating flight itself has begun, neither dragon will eat again for a period of several years.

Courtship behavior is colorful in most animal species. It is extravagantly exuberant in dragons. The mating pair display the full range of their flying and swimming ability in concert and as solo performances. Though all dragon flight is beautiful, performances during the mating period exceed any others. The pair are very noisy, using both the bellow and the percussive language to the fullest extent. Active displays give way to brief periods of rest on the ocean surface, or on snow, only to erupt suddenly into more violent acrobatics. Nightlife came to a standstill in Crested Butte, Colorado, and its ski resorts last January when the pair of mating dragons who had spent the afternoon spying from an aspen woods by the major trail, turned the slopes into fire slides and lighted the surrounding mountain peaks with their incandescent dances (*Denver Post*).

Although we know that the eggs are fertilized internally (Grenner and Del Rio, RevZoo 14:7:4), we do not know how this is accomplished. So far it has been impossible to determine if the male anatomy includes an intromittent organ. Pairs have been observed rising vertically from the sea with ventral surfaces touching from jaw to tail before peeling apart in wide arcs tens of meters in the air. This would appear to be the mating position; however, the same pattern is often repeated with dorsal surfaces in contact. In short, we do not know if the actual mating occurs in the air or under water, or if it occurs once or several times. Once mating is complete, however, the pair return to nearly normal behavior (St. James, NZSDSWP 7). The period between mating and the laying of eggs is spent in what can only be described as 'fond companionship', the pair grooming one another and sharing relaxed observation and swimming (St. James, NZSDSWP 7).

Incubation and the Hatch

At present we do not know the duration of either the internal or external incubation period, since the entire process has not been observed. The research team of Wanda Grenner and Serafin Del Rio watched a pair take turns guarding eggs for six weeks, so it is safe to assume that the eggs are laid at least six weeks before they hatch, but that is as much information as we have (Grenner and Del Rio, AnatLat XII: 8). (An excerpt from correspondence from this team appears below).

During the internal incubation period the pair select the hatching area and defend it against any intrusion. The hatching area is secluded and quite small, only 10 to 20 meters square, so that the adults are crowded after the eggs are laid.

This serves to keep the temperature elevated and creates an informal incubator. The parents take turns guarding the eggs, coiling around them until they are completely covered. Several times a day each egg is subjected to direct fire for several minutes. There are five to nine eggs in a hatch. The eggs are large, about 35 centimeters from pole to pole and roughly the same in diameter. The shells fall roughly into two groups: what is called the Atlantic type, opalescent with a pink cast; and the Asian, which is more silver, with a metallic sheen, marked at the poles with faint crimson streaks. Del Rio found both types in the same hatch (Grenner and Del Rio, RevZoo 14). He and Grenner recovered shell fragments and had them subjected to petrological analysis, which indicated that the shell has the density and tensile strength of granite (Grenner and Del Rio, AnatLat XII: 8).

When the rustling of the kits can be heard inside the shell, the female pierces the egg with her incisors and bites firmly until the shell breaks apart, exposing the young kit to the air. This task requires a subtle balance of brute strength and fine judgment, since the shell is from 2 to 3 centimeters thick and the kit is in contact with the shell at all points.

The newly hatched kits are fed immediately. When all the eggs are hatched, the kits are gathered up and carried off in their parents' mouths to a larger area, the 'cache', which has been selected and guarded during the incubation period. After the kits have been released, the male tramples the fragments of shell into fine sand, which he mixes with the dirt of the hatching area. Predators and curious primates visit the hatching area repeatedly for several days after the departure of the dragons, which probably accounts for the destruction of shell fragments and the elaborate air transportation of the kits to the cache.

The following is an excerpt from a letter to the author from Wanda Grenner describing one field trip that she and Serafin Del Rio made in search of infant kits. On this expedition along the upper reaches of the Rio Neuguén in southwestern Argentina, they found the hatch that provided the information forming the basis for all their studies on hatching and infant kits.

We watched Espantosa [the female] open the eggs, cocking her head attentively to each one, cupping it close to her ear to see if it was ready to break. Margarito [the male] was very excited during this procedure. He talked constantly, in the liquid dragon language, crooning and conversing. We would have given a great deal to be able to understand him, as you can imagine. As each egg broke, he would lean close to see, talking excitedly. If the egg was not ready to open, he took it back from Espantosa and tucked it under his foreleg again. If she judged it ready, she put it in her mouth, bracing it with her canines. We were astounded, actually, when she put the first egg in her mouth. She'd been out of sorts all day, and we feared that she was going to destroy the whole hatch. But she didn't. She closed her jaws slowly, firmly, until the shell shattered with a clear ring, leaving the kit wiggling on her tongue. The tiny kit would slide head-down into her throat and drink. Espantosa would lay her head gently on the ground, and the kit would clamber out and scamper under Margarito's leg.

Their scales were quite soft when they first came out of the shell, and kind of wrinkled. They looked like grey tissue-paper dragons. Within minutes, though, the scales had flattened and toughened to what must have been the consistency of vulcanized rubber – they would take an impression, but would not keep it, and the kits could move across a sharp surface, like Margarito's teeth, without flinching. We could see the sun through their bodies, and even could make out the tiny skeletons. They were sleeker than adults or even older kits. Their heads didn't have horns or foreknobs, and the collar and wings were folded close.

They didn't stay under Margarito's leg quietly. They would peek out around his elbow or between his claws, or scramble out as he took out an unbroken egg. By the time the last kit was hatched, the miniature roil was crawling all over the tangled pile of parent bodies, peering into Espantosa's mouth, hanging over eyes, sliding down necks, clinging to chins and horns. The wings opened almost accidentally. If the kit slipped, he would jerk his wings suddenly to catch himself and there he was – winged. We could see the webbing lose transparency as it hardened in the air. They clung with their claws to Margarito's lower jaw, swinging in the motion of his head, spreading their wings and collars. There were eight in all – a dark green and black brindle; two purple and rust, a medium grey, who sprouted horns as we watched; a darker brown-grey with dark brown stripes; one about the color of the Atlantic at four p.m. in January on Long Island; a clear grey, and a lovely little sand-colored one with green markings.

When all the eggs were hatched, and each kit had eaten at least twice – a period of two hours at the most – all the kits clambered into their parents' mouths. Espantosa had four and Margarito the other four. They flew off to the southeast: the tails of the kits hanging free, heads poking out from between the teeth. It made a memorable sight. They did not return to the hatching area.

A portion of the letter describing shell fragments and other minutiae from the hatch area is omitted. The letter continues:

Although the cache was really quite close by, we had a hard time finding it and wasted an entire day searching southeast, when the cache was really a mile and a half to the northwest. We finally located it by reasoning that Espantosa and Margarito expected us to follow them. They had ignored us during the entire six weeks' vigil at the hatch. They knew we were there: they never looked in our direction and avoided coming our way, but since we were content to be unobtrusive spectators, they tolerated us. I don't know really why they put up with us. But watching at the hatch was one thing, and being at the cache itself was quite another matter. When Espantosa spotted us, long before we even knew we were close, she alerted Margarito. We heard her snuffle. He drove us off. He came at us, crawling slowly on his belly, low with his collar up, making a moaning grumble that was truly terrifying. We gave ground, politely, we thought, but he wanted more than politeness, and leapt into the air, cupping his wings and compressing his body so that the scales stood straight out. He herded us away from the cache, making us run and walk as fast as we could over that terrain for what seemed like hours, though it was probably only an hour and a half. By jerking his wings suddenly, he could knock us off our feet with a great gust of wind if he thought we showed signs of stopping. When we had climbed over a hill and were slithering down a large skree, he alighted and watched us descend in a jumble of rocks and dust. Whenever we looked back as we walked away from the hill, he belched fire at us and screeched. We camped, rather disconsolate, a good twenty miles on foot from the cache. Along the Neuguén, 30 kilometers on foot is no joke. Two days later we began to make our way back to the cache, circling around through dense undergrowth for hours and hours. When we made our turn and faced the cache again, a grove of trees burst into flame, not ten feet in front of us. Margarito hung in the air over our heads, making an earsplitting whining scream that left us dazed and deafened. When we turned away from the cache, he stopped. He floated above our heads while the fire raged behind us, and our ears burned painfully from the shriek. If we stopped walking, he would blow scalding air around us, and if we even looked over our shoulders, he began that incredible shrieking again. Margarito flew off, though he checked up on us three or four times a day while we made up our minds that there was no hope of continuing our study of that family. We would see him low on the horizon, zigzagging until he spotted us. When he was satisfied that we were still moving away, he would fly off. The last time we saw him was just before we reached Neuguén. He flew directly over us. We were dismayed to see him flying at us, but he paused briefly in midair and made a soft, breathy sigh, 'HO', that seemed so full of kindness we both wept. When I described that noise to Marsden years later, he took an enormous breath and repeated it. Extraordinary. It brought tears to my eyes instantly. He couldn't reproduce the resonance, of course, but the intonation was exact. He wouldn't tell me what the sound meant. 'It meant what you heard', was all he would say.

The Cache

The area where the young are raised is called the cache. Dragons nurture their young in a temperate climate, between 5 and 30 degrees C, where there is frequent rainfall and plenty of sun. Since dragons like to have seclusion but ready access to water for the kits, caches are located near the sea or on an inlet or estuary, though river caches are not uncommon. They like to have a ready supply of food near at hand, both fish and meat, as well as assorted vegetables. The chart below

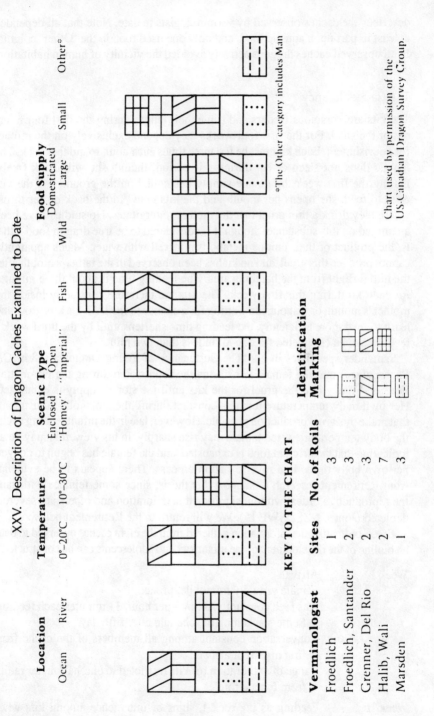

XXV. Description of Dragon Caches Examined to Date

Chart used by permission of the US-Canadian Dragon Survey Group.

*The Other category includes Man

describes the caches observed by verminologists to date. Note that all depended at least in part upon aquatic food, and only one used food in the 'Other' column. In all observed caches dragons actively avoided the vicinity of human habitation.

The Cache: Infancy

The kits are voracious feeders and triple their length during the first four hours out of the shell. For the first four weeks they depend exclusively on the mother for nourishment. Each kit must be fed three times each hour, round the clock. The female does not sleep or eat during this period, though she will drink freely. During the first week the female simply lies coiled on the ground. As the kits need to feed, she opens her mouth and the kits crawl to the back of her throat where they drink a thin gruel that the mother regurgitates. No studies have been attempted on this substance, though it is considered to be true dragon food – that is, the product of their unique metabolism mixed with water. Males apparently cannot produce this gruel, and no kit has been observed in the father's mouth after the initial flight from the hatching area. The feeding time is about three minutes for each kit during this first week. The kits are therefore constantly inside the mother's mouth, or just outside waiting for a chance to feed. As the kits grow and learn to feed more efficiently, the feeding time shortens until by the third week a feeding can be completed for one kit in less than two minutes.

Santander speculates in his 'The Sustenance of Young Dragons' (58th ICA *Proceedings*) that the female transforms the food stored during the pre-mating Feeding Frenzy into the gruel for the kits until the stored supply is exhausted. Her own body temperature remains constant during the metabolic adjustments that make this gruel production possible. However, late in the infant feeding cycle, the body temperature of the female may rise sharply. In his view, this may be an indication that the original food is exhausted, and the female has begun to convert her own body tissue in a reverse fusion process. There appears to be evidence from Retirement research to support this thesis, since some females withstand the reproductive ordeal without significant deterioration and others are severely depleted (Jones, NZSDSWP 15). We will return to the Retirement below.

By co-ordinating the information gathered from the eight caches observed to date, an outline of the development of the infant kits into adolescents can be constructed.

Week I	Arrival.
	Female virtually immobile, prone.
	Kits feed constantly, 3 times per hour, 3+ minutes each feeding. Some slackening of schedule after fifth day.
	Conversation constant among all members of the cache from first instant of arrival.
	Range of exploration for kits restricted to one-half meter radius from female foreleg.
Week II	Feeding as in Week I, signs of impatience among kits when feeding turns are delayed.

After day 10 female drinks for 3 minutes, twice each 24 hours.

Male talks individually to each kit, encouraging it to explore beyond area around female foreleg.

Range of exploration, full length of female out to 2 meters.

Week III Feedings as in Week I, each feeding no less than 3 minutes.

Female shifts position more frequently, luring kits into new territory. After day 19, interrupts feeding schedule 4 times daily for drink of water.

Kits start to mimic percussive language in earnest. Sounds of endearment – attempt at steamy sigh, strike earth with tails to express impatience. Some irritation from adults. Learn to run steadily with wings outspread. After day 15 flap wings while running. Learn rudiments of ground Knots. Join in Chants. First bellow after day 21.

Male takes individual kits for short explorations of new territory.

Range of exploration, unaccompanied, 6 meters, increasing.

Week IV Feed 3 times each hour for about 1.5 minutes. After day 24 male introduces solid food – small game and fish.

Female drinks at will, shifts position freely. Kits learn to drink while she is upright.

Begin to teach moderation in use of percussive language; bellow reaches full pre-adolescent development; Knot games fully elaborated on ground: arrange spatially, use both abstract and representational designs. Chant with the group regularly, kits Chant as a group without adults.

Each kit taken individually into deep water. Wings now sufficiently developed to support weight. First attempts at flying.

Range of exploration 300+ meters, area marked by adults.

Weeks V, VI Feeding 3 times per hour, 1–1.5 minutes. Small quantities of solid food taken daily, increasing.

Percussive language 40 percent, hindered by lack of steam. Knots transferred to water. First signs of play hoarding and king-of-the-pile. Knot and Chant with adults.

Flying, swimming, and exploration in earnest. All kits fly freely over the cache at low altitude.

Weeks VII–IX Feeding 2 times per hour, 1–1.5 minutes.

Knot games transferred to air; discrimination in selection of items for play hoard. Male and female begin to teach stalking and silence.

Weeks X–XI Feeding dwindles to once an hour, 1–1.5 minutes per feeding.

Female begins to show signs of depletion. By end of period more than 50 percent of food intake is solid food, some self-caught.

Kits master stalking skills, always in group. Range freely.

Male leaves cache for up to one week on a solo hunting trip.

Weeks XII–XIV   Kits continue to feed at will. Interval lengthens dramatically as they learn to take their own meals from environment. Continue to feed at least twice a day as long as female is in the cache. Lower temperatures induce more frequent feeding.
Use of percussive language is encouraged by both adults.
Kits are almost self-sufficient by the end of the week XIII.

Week XV+   Depending on temperature and needs of kits, female goes into Retirement.

Retirement and the Survival of Females after Reproduction

When the female leaves the young kits, she is almost exhausted. She has not eaten during the entire procreation period, having stored all her nourishment during the preparation for the mating flight, more than a year before the actual hatching. She retires in a most literal sense to a remote spot where food is plentiful and easily caught and where there is no danger of attack. She grazes in a leisurely fashion for one-and-a-half to two years, replenishing her reserves and rebuilding her strength before resuming the Wandering. During the Retirement the female dragon must be able to consume in the neighborhood of five hundred kilograms of varied foodstuffs daily. The sea, therefore, makes a natural refuge, where game is abundantly available and where she may hunt by swimming, which takes less effort than flying or crawling. The ocean off the Bermuda Rise is a favorite haunt of females in this condition, as is the Gulf Stream throughout its course, the Tasman Sea, and the rich fishing areas south of the Aleutian chain.

The most extensive research on females in Retirement has been conducted by Sean Jones, who has spent years drifting between Cape Howe and Great Sandy Island in the East Australian Current in his ship, the *Liliana*. Though the population of females in the Tasman Sea is high, they are so wary during the Retirement that Jones does not sight more than five specimens during any four-month period of searching. Data on Retirement, then, is perhaps even harder to compile than that on kits. (Jones publishes regularly in the New Zealand School of Dragon Studies publications. Material for this introduction to the Retirement is drawn from his contributions to the *Working Papers*).

Jones divides the Retirement into three stages: Retreat, Preliminary Recovery, and Recuperation. The Retreat begins when the female leaves the cache. Under the best conditions this journey is extremely perilous because of her depleted energy. She is in fact starving. An unwary female may be taken alive during the first two days of her retreat if she is particularly spent and has been forced to reconstruct food for the roil from her own body tissue in the reversed fusion process. If taken, she will not submit to captivity, of course, but will destroy herself and all around her within minutes of capture.

The library of the New Zealand School of Dragon Studies has a remarkable film taken by William Thompson and Richard L. Chu off the coast of Greenland.

The film was made forty years ago when the existence of dragons was still mere hearsay in some areas. Thompson and Chu were conducting an oceanographic survey of the northeastern coast of Greenland for the University of Aberdeen. Late one afternoon to their surprise they spotted a dragon flying toward their vessel. Thompson started filming the dragon as she approached.

The film shows a severe case of post-procreative depletion. The flight of the dragon is listless. She clearly does not notice the small ship with its out-riggers of exploratory gear. This in itself is an indication of extreme exhaustion. She flies straight for the beach of the nearby island without a preliminary scouting pass, and does not change position after landfall. The vessels in her wings are indistinct, and although it is near dusk, there is only a faint glow about the head, indicating a very low metabolic rate. After this portion of the film was made, Chu prudently ordered the ship into the open sea for the night, well away from the cove.

The next morning curiosity and Thompson's valuable scientific obsession with recording every phenomenon brought them within telescopic range of the beast. She remained in the same position they had filmed the night before, and she was still immobile at noon. The expedition continued with the mapping of the sea floor on the coast until evening. When the dragon proved to be in the same position at 7:00 p.m. and no movement came in response to flares exploded near her on the beach, they decided – unwisely – that the dragon was dead. This was, after all, an expedition of oceanographers, verminology was in its infancy, and very little factual information about dragons was available even to educated people.

Thompson decided to go ashore to photograph at close range and to look into the possibility of salvaging the carcass. Chu, who was better read and more cautious by nature, flatly opposed the plan. However, when an hour's observation at close range showed no movement except a gull walking over the inert dragon's tail, Thompson insisted and put to shore in the landing craft, taking two assistants with portable cameras and collecting gear. Chu, in agonized silence, filmed the encounter from the ship.

The noise of the small boat motor did not wake the dragon, nor did the preliminary work with the still camera. Thompson and his first assistant, Cleve-land Verbecki, worked within arm's length of the dragon, photographing methodi-cally meter by meter from the tail forward. They were able to photograph the entire beast, taking special care at the head and forequarters. The reflex action of the stereographex is inaudible to human ears and did not rouse the dragon. Gene Grouse, Thompson's other assistant, proceeding cautiously, completed detailed measurements, including the lifting of individual scales in his callipers. Appar-ently, the metabolic rate was so low that they did not encounter any noticeable heat from the body. At this point, Chu's film shows Verbecki and Grouse collecting gear and heading back to the craft. Thompson gestures wildly to them. A lively argument follows. Close examination of the film with the stop-frame technique shows the dragon's eye opening, observing, and closing during the argument, although she does not move except for a slight tremor in the tail.

Thompson breaks from the group with the exasperated flailing of the arms his students knew too well, and proceeds to shove at the dragon with both hands and a foot in what is apparently an effort to roll her over on her side so that he may photograph the ventral surface. The dragon gasps, belches, gasps and explodes in the spectacular fireball that concludes this remarkable and tragic film.[3] Richard Chu sent the film to Marsden with the question, Why was the dragon so passive? Jones identified the condition of the dragon. It was the first reliable evidence of the violent toll reproduction takes on the female. It is also a graphic demonstration of the importance of a basic general knowledge of dragons to anyone venturing into areas where they may be present.

After the female has reached refuge, the second phase begins: Preliminary Recovery. This stage lasts from three to four weeks. The female divides her time between active foraging and sleeping on the sea floor. The foraging is intense, although there is none of the exuberant abandon of the pre-mating Frenzy. She eats rapidly and without consideration, ingesting animal and vegetable sources with equal voraciousness for two hours at a stretch. She will, in fact, eat with a deliberate thoroughness any living non-dragon entity that comes into her path. Jones has watched female dragons swim through schools of fish with their mouths open, catching and swallowing in the same motion. Sharks attracted by the kill suffer the same fate as lesser prey. During the Preliminary Recovery period she stays to herself, concentrating on the pressing task of filling herself to capacity at least three times a day (Jones, NZSDSWP 2).

When her strength begins to return, she seeks company of other females in the same Retirement grounds. They do not interact openly, but sleep and feed in the same general area and bask together. This is the Recuperation, which can last from one to three years. When a dragon is completely recovered, she will resume the Wandering. By using heat-sensitive gear aboard the *Liliana*, Jones has located groups of females drifting in warm currents just below the surface of the sea, completely in mime (NZSDSWP 15).

Below is an excerpt of a letter from Jones to Marsden describing an encounter with a group of female dragons (letter used by permission). It presents Jones's field study method and gives a good indication of the lassitude of these beasts during the Recuperation.

> At daybreak I floated into a group of females resting on the surface. I was on the raft that day – the *Wormwood*, as we call it – and had cut the motor as soon as I was well away from the *Liliana*. We have found the raft the least offensive means of transportation on the open sea. (Least offensive to them). They don't like aqualungs – the bubbling is too close to percussive bubbling, I think, and annoys them by sounding as if it almost means something. Motors offend their sense of dignity. They tolerate sails. I had a funny run-in once with three playful worms who mimicked

---

[3] At the request of the families, this film is not available for public use, and has not been shown outside the School.

the sounds of my sheets with their wings, and came about when I did with a great flocking racket. Dragons have liked my canoe, partly because they can upset it easily and enjoy watching me try to right it – but it is not suited to deep-water work on the open sea. So we have devised this raft, the one I was riding on that day, to suit our minimal needs and their plentiful idiosyncrasies.

This group accepted me as part of the scene. They looked almost like giant seaweed: varying shades of green, blue, and brown, completely limp. They rode the waves three-quarters submerged. There were five in the group, spread out over an area about the size of two football fields. They took the waves head on or aslant, their flaccid bodies exactly following the crests and trenches. One, a bottle-green and rust with deep brown brindling, kept her side to the wind by using her wings as sculls. The rising waves would occasionally lift her wing from the water and drop it back with a soft smack. That was the only sound. They allowed me to drift among them. In the group was a dragon I recognized, the small green with the branching horns who had dived away from us the month before while we were off Cape Howe. I had guessed then that she was a new arrival. I lay on my stomach a long time that morning, holding the tiller with my feet and legs – eye-to-eye with enough dragons to satisfy even my curiosity for the moment. As the sun got well up, they sank lower and lower beneath the surface until I lost sight of them.

The Cache: The Young Kit

The female remains with the cache until each kit is able to catch a major portion of its own food. With her Retreat, withdrawal of the supply of dragon fuel triggers the beginning of the development of the fire chamber. The inception of the transformation from ordinary to dragon digestion is apparent five months after weaning, when the body temperature begins to rise (Santander, 58th ICA *Proceedings*). The kits continue to eat several times a day and to defecate frequently for three years while the development of the chamber is incomplete and they depend on the less efficient metabolism of their young years. The kits are now in effect no more dangerous than other large and voracious carnivores. As the first chamber develops, however, they assume the further lethal dimension appropriate to their kind: fire, augmented by the mime (Froedlich, ABD, 254).

While the kits are in infancy they cannot mime. The adults do not mime in their presence unless necessary for defense of the cache. They accommodate the young: they remain visible, just as they converse vocally. When the kits have mastered the percussive vocabulary, the use of vocal communication falls to a 25 percent level, reserved for instruction and exhortation. Similarly, as the ability to mime develops, the adult resumes his normal mimic behavior. The roil learns mimicking skills through playing hide-and-seek, with the male joining as the master. He teaches them the advantages of miming in the hunt, and shows them

XXVI. Three young dragons racing across the Susquehanna River south of Sunbury,
Pennsylvania, leave paths of broken ice floating in open water.
(*Photo: Gregory Lucas*)

the usefulness of heat in attracting game, especially aquatic prey (Froedlich,
ABD, 230).

When the female leaves on the Retreat, the kits are a little less than half their
full size. They grow slowly during the succeeding years until the fire chamber is
sufficiently developed to begin supplying true dragon food. When the process is
nearly complete, their body heat can be measured at nearly adult levels, and they
begin the final growth, gaining both length and weight very rapidly. Six months
after the fire chamber is fully functional, the kit has achieved his full length and
close to his full weight. The kits are then 'stern' and 'stiera', some four-and-a-half
to five years after hatching, depending on conditions (Liu, CompBlgy 23:7).

The fully self-sufficient stern and stiera remain in the cache with the adult male
for many years. On Ascension Marsden observed the first roil in this stage of
development for fifteen years. In five of the observed caches, an adult dragon
joined a group that had included only one adult. Presumably these were the
original females, returning after Retirement (Halib and Wali, DNDI:OP 3).
Marsden observed that even after the roil had dispersed, the adults remained in

the cache with the remaining roil and parents, in a loose confederation, sharing some of the teaching tasks, and joining in the Chants and Knot games as they had before the first group left. Parents, adults, and roil appear to enjoy proximity. (The record of Marsden's field study on Ascension, as it pertains to the development of the roil, is available in his contributions to NZSDSWP 6 and 18).

During this long period of adolescence the dragons of the cache, adults and roil, continue to spend most of their time in company. They hunt in groups, spend long hours constructing elaborate Knot patterns on the ground and in the air, and pass the nights in chanting. Froedlich and Santander watched fourteen dragons, adult and stern, for three hours flying through a series of languid three-dimensional constructions hundreds of meters in the air (Froedlich and Santander, NZSDSWP 3 as recorded by Marsden). According to Marsden, the first roil on Ascension left suddenly without any prior discussion or preparation that he could discern. They spent an ordinary evening swimming and chanting, and at dawn they simply flew off, the group dispersing as it gained altitude. On the island, life for the remaining dragons went on as before (Marsden, NZSDSWP 6).

Apparently dragon affection is not bonded to physical presence. Throughout the procreative cycle the dragons are openly affectionate with each other, rubbing, grooming, and performing acts of consideration. The adults display unfailing fondness and remarkable patience with the kits. Dragons part without clamor, however. The female leaves, as she must to survive, and the remaining dragons accept her departure calmly and continue the daily routine. If she returns, she is accepted without ceremony into the group. The kits disperse without ceremonies of anticipation or regret. Perhaps parting loses much of its sting without the prospect of imminent death, which colors human relationships.

Froedlich's Experience with the Roils of Taitao

Perhaps the most appropriate description of the life of young dragons can be drawn from the experiences of Marta Froedlich, who was the first person of the Modern Infestation Period to see dragon kits. In fact, for twenty years, until her student, Philip Marsden, established his base on Ascension Island, she remained the only person to accomplish a firsthand study of dragons before Wandering. Her published reports on the six months she spent with the three roils she encountered on the west coast of Chile are professional in tone, as are Marsden's. In print, and at scientific meetings, she never discussed the experience of living in close proximity to kits, believing, perhaps with good reason, that her campaign to have dragon studies accepted as a serious science would not be helped by the rather unusual nature of her encounter. However, an account of that first meeting is appropriate for this introductory book, because it conveys the total atmosphere of the cache, complete with three roils of different ages. Froedlich's experience is unique: as far as we know, though many caches have been studied, no one else has ever been included in the daily activities as an accepted member of the cache.

What follows is an edited transcription of a tape made by Emilio Branco, a close friend of Froedlich's, and Luc Maria Santander, the wife of Froedlich's longtime companion and collaborator, Baodelio Santander. The transcription is quoted at length because the material loses its flavor if it is reduced or rewritten, and the quality of the experience is important in understanding the life of the cache. On this tape Sr. Branco and Sra. Santander are remembering what Marta Froedlich had told them about her work on the Taitao Peninsula. She went to Paposo at twenty-six, a year before the Stewart Island incident. At that time the educated population of the world was not convinced that dragons existed at all. Froedlich herself was skeptical. She went to the west coast of Chile for a field study of small lizards, a kind of gecko.

> Marta was very lightly equipped. She meant to be in the field only a few weeks, and it was the beginning of the warm season. She had her typewriter, some recording equipment, and a backpack. She took a two-way radio only because she was forced to. Even at this time, when she was only in her mid-twenties, Marta was quite independent and ready to be completely on her own in the field. She was always self-sufficient, and the problems of surviving alone in the rugged, rather hostile country never seemed to daunt her. When Baodelio went back there with her on the second trip, he was appalled that she had even thought of making the trip alone. It is quite wild there, but Marta trudged along oblivious of the dangers of the situation. She always went on foot as much as possible, of course.
>
> One morning she traveled into an area near Paposo that had not been studied for many years. She had left the last village behind the previous afternoon, so she was surprised to hear an unfamiliar sound: 'not unlike rapidly boiling water, punctuated by squeaks, clicks, and groans'. She proceeded cautiously, seeking the source of what she called 'that incessant burbling'. Pulling her way up a long rise on her elbows, she peered over into a sheltered valley that opened into the sea.
>
> The little valley was home to three roils. One roil was playing in the air as she came over the crest of the hill, making the intricate patterns of the Knot game – 'dragon lace', Marta called it. A second was scattered here and there on the ground, exploring. [The third was transported into the valley two days later]. It was like a party, she said; there was an air of excitement and exuberant delight that persisted throughout her six months' stay. The sound that had attracted her was the normal noise of a cache with kits. They chatter almost constantly from the instant they are born. They talk to one another, to their parents, to anything that will listen or appear to. They hold earnest, one-sided conversations with plants and inanimate objects and become enraged when there is no response. The vegetation around the roil suffers until the kits learn to select a responsive listener.
>
> In addition to the incessant chattering, the kits are constantly exploring. Marta speculated that the kits she observed made physical contact with every foot of their territory every day, touching or brushing every surface

with every portion of their bodies. They twisted, curled, slipped past one another, making elaborate Knots, singly or in groups, escaping from them, always in motion. Baodelio said he sometimes got dizzy watching dragons, especially if he was looking down on them, and he and Marta saw only four in a group when they went back there on that second trip. She was watching lots of them. As they mastered flying, she watched them transfer the knotting games to the air, and elaborate them into three dimensions. The kits from the roils visited each other freely, and the parents enjoyed the convivial atmosphere as thoroughly as the young. The kits fought freely, too, over territory, over prey, over games, over practice hoards, or for no reason – in the air, on the beach, in the valley, in the sea.

The oldest roil discovered Marta as she inched her way cautiously over the crest of the hill overlooking the valley. They flew over her, brushing her with their wings and tails, talking to each other rapidly – 'chortling' is what she called it later, but she didn't feel particularly sanguine about it all at the time. The younger kits quickly joined them. Before she knew what was happening, she found herself bowled over and buried under their swift, twisting bodies: 'boiled in snakes' is how she described it. She was terrified, of course, and nearly smothered. But the absurdity of the situation broke in on her when she found herself staring into an enormous curious eye. She was susceptible to absurdity, Marta was, and she was always laughing at something. She began to laugh then and shout back at them, which they enjoyed. They adopted her as a pet instantly. They would drag her out of her tent to tickle her or to carry her along on excursions. She learned quickly not to resist them, and although they were rough with her sometimes, they never hurt her or dropped her while they were flying, except from low heights into the sea. The clumsiness of human swimming amused them, and they appeared to enjoy the splash as she hit the water.

The parents tolerated her. When she first encountered the kits, or when they encountered her, she did not see the adults. She said that they had probably gone into mime when they had sensed her approaching the valley. After the kits had finished exploring her, she noticed the parents, one quite close by – 'about that far away from my hand' – and the others resting in the valley and on the beach. Even years afterward, when she was on friendly terms with dragons, she would still shut her eyes when she spoke of that first face-to-face meeting with a full-grown dragon. The adults did not threaten her then and subsequently never attempted to intervene between the kits and their pet.

The kits seldom played with her while they were in the company of their parents, though she was free to move about as she pleased and could watch them take their swimming lessons. Occasionally she would be taken along on a hunting foray or brought into the cache when the kits were ready to bed down for the night with one parent or the other. The parent would ignore her on these occasions, including her impartially under a protecting wing. At first she tried to keep perfectly still. The foreleg of an adult dragon being two meters long, she was aware of the precariousness of her position. But as time went on, she relaxed and learned to doze. The warmth of the cache was welcome as summer ended.

Once she was taken along on a hunting trip, when the second roil was being taught how to steal goats from the fringes of a tended herd. As she sat absolutely still where the kit had set her down behind a boulder, the parent noticed her, staring straight into her eyes. It gave her an 'extraordinary sensation', she said. 'It was a long, searching look, aloof, full of profound amusement and a lively, intelligent understanding of exactly who I was'. She did not fear the parents after that incident, but she was always aware of their presence by a prickling sensation at the nape of her neck. Baodelio said he could always tell when they were going to meet Jim or Rosa unexpectedly by the gooseflesh rising on Marta's arms.

During this first time Marta didn't learn dragon speech. That came much later when Philip and Philomel went to Cananéia. She did learn to mimic some of their sounds, which amused them, but she did not understand them. For their part, the kits didn't appear to pay attention to her noises, though one kit, Rosa, would imitate her when she muttered to herself. Marta always muttered. It came from living alone, she said. A few weeks after she was taken up by the community, she was startled to hear the kits shouting, 'Help, oh, help, get off me', very distinctly to one another as they boiled up the hill to get her. They all learned to say, 'Stop tickling me, you nasty worm', and would tease her by shouting it as they tickled her or by whispering it into her tent at night. But they never conversed with her. They liked the sound of her typewriter and learned to reproduce the noise. The parents also came to make that sound, and the community adopted it as her name. When the sound of a typewriter at 80 words per minute entered the general burble, she learned to be alert for visitors. The machine itself was broken the third day when it refused to answer Mateo, who had talked earnestly to it for five minutes. The two-way radio they dropped into the sea the first afternoon.

Her things had a way of disappearing into their play hoards: combs, socks, pens, her other set of clothes. At the end of six months she had very little left. The only time she ever felt in danger with them was once when the oldest kits were playing hoard and she was the booty. 'I felt like a fool, sitting on top of a pile of rocks and twigs like some roosting gull', she said. 'But then they began to fight over me, and Mateo came flying over and landed on top of me with his full weight smashed onto my back'. It was the only time she thought they had actually forgotten what she was. When the game seemed to be cooling off she poked his stomach with her free elbow until he moved. He was abashed and straightened out her arms and legs very solicitously, peering into her face and gurgling gently.

They were delighted with her daily routine. Dressing was hilarious. They would take her shoes off, or drop her into the ocean so they could watch her change clothes. Since she had only one change along, she was often trying to get into wet khakis, knowing perfectly well that as soon as she got them on, she'd be carried out to sea again. They would collect piles of sticks and twigs in hope she would make a fire – an activity that was as interesting to them as her swimming. They learned her food preferences and would bring her red snapper or mackerel or take her to places where she could find the fruits and vegetables she liked best. They would say 'ah' and 'um' encouragingly, and were very proud of her when she ate their presents. They learned that if she started to undo her belt she needed to be taken out of the cache, or to be put down on the ground, and would wait quietly until she was through.

But the best times, she said, were the Chants, even though they often left her deaf for days. The adults would start things off with a preparatory hum or two. Then they would all burst into bellows. Marta just lay out flat and took it in, quivering along with the ground itself. The youngest kits couldn't bellow, but they would trill away. The Chants left her limp. 'If they ever wanted to squash me without my even being aware of it, those were the times to do it'.

As the kits got older and the last group learned to fly, they began to lose interest in her, except for Rosa and Jim, who remained her friends and would check up on her from time to time. She saw those two off and on for the rest of her life. They would appear suddenly in the vicinity of her field station and stay around for a few days, clicking at her occasionally. They even made appearances outside her office window at the University of São Paulo. The University can't really be blamed for being alarmed. When Baodelio was with her at Cananéia both Jim and Rosa spent a lot of time with them.

Jim even came looking for her while she was in residence at Yale University in the United States. He astonished the staff at the Bienecke Library by staring in through the front entrance early one December afternoon. After he located her office he remained in New Haven three days, spending most of his time floating in the harbor. Marta seized this opportunity and rented a small boat for herself. She took along her most promising student – 'a real find', she called him. Philip was a graduate student in anthropology at the time and had fallen in with her. Jim apparently understood Marta's intention and allowed the two of them to accompany him in the harbor during the late afternoons – the three of them resting quietly on the water.

There is no question about the importance of Froedlich's chance meeting with the dragons on the Taitao Peninsula. It formed the foundation for the scientific investigation of dragons and provided the opportunity for the recruitment of Philip Marsden to the field. It is most generous of Dr. Branco and Sra. Santander to share these private insights. Froedlich's stature as a verminologist cannot be lessened now by a general knowledge of her informal initiation into the field.

Longevity

We do not have enough information to establish the normal dragon lifespan. To determine an average longevity, we must be able to record the birth and death from natural causes of a respectable number of individuals. To date we have reliable information about the births, or very early lives of a number of dragons, and we have records of two dragon deaths: the female who died while Thompson was attempting to examine her and an adult male who was killed by the San Cristóbal dragon in the attempt to steal his hoard (Lucan, *The Destruction of San Cristóbal*, 176). Sean Jones has established that after procreation females are vulnerable, but he has reported no deaths (Jones, NZSDSWP 12). Presumably dragons do, or will, die of natural causes, including the complications of the degeneration of old age. However, at present we know nothing about dragon death.

Although an individual dragon or a small group may be observed for a period of time in one location, the same dragon is rarely sighted a second time once he has left the original site. Of the forty-five dragons Marsden saw more than ten times during his stay on Ascension, he learned to make instantaneous identification of thirty-three. Six were adult dragons who used Ascension as an observation site on and off during his time there. He considered himself intimately familiar with the thirteen kits of the roil born in the third month after his arrival on Ascension. He saw these kits daily for seventeen years and could recognize them by sound as well as by sight, a portion of tail or foot being enough evidence for positive identification. Five of them he could identify by smell alone. He was almost as familiar with the eight kits of the second roil, the two parent pairs and two adult dragons who stayed on Ascension during the first seven years of his study. Since both of the latter were growing, he assumed that they were two of a previous roil, most of which had already set out on the Wandering. However, even given this familiarity, Marsden never succeeded in making a positive identification of even one of these thirty-three dragons after he left Ascension, though he remained active in the field for the rest of his life, an additional forty-two years.

Shortly after leaving Ascension he did make two tentative identifications of young dragons in flight as he was on board outbound from the island, and a third, twenty-two years later, as he put ashore on a small island in the Aleutians. Here, he flushed a young female from some 270 meters inland. She did not reappear, and he had no camera at hand as he beached his craft. However, he was reasonably certain that this dragon was the kit whom he had called Grace on Ascension (Marsden, NZSDSWP 11). Only Froedlich herself can be said to have had a lifelong association with individual dragons, and that was not due to her initiative. The dragons sought her out.

A program of dragon monitoring could be established if individual dragons could be fitted with permanent marking. Forty years ago a small team from the Penfirth University Center received federal funding for a project that sought to fit yearling kits with radio transmitters by winning their parents to the plan. When

XXVII. Gulkana Glacier, Alaska. A pair of dragons make their way across the
glacier. The melting pattern shows that this is not their first trip. Marsden was
called to locate and identify these dragons, but was unable to do so.
(*Photo: George B. Wharton, Jr*)

a young roil was spotted on Sanak Island, the expedition set out from Penfirth
with four people from the center and a poet-consultant. However, there was no
word from the expedition after eight days, and the plan was abandoned.

Rubsen's accounts of his attempt at dragon marking are sufficiently discouraging to dispel any hope of devising a tag system using present technology.
Sophisticated radiation, laser, and niploid techniques were defeated by wariness,
speed, and mimicry over a period of twelve years, despite many thousands of
dollars' worth of equipment and impressive ingenuity on Rubsen's part. His fatal
attempt to tag the dragon of the Andreanof Islands by running at his tail with an
orange tag mounted on a harpoon is perhaps all that needs to be said about this
particular field of dragon study and the despair that it engenders (Rubsen and
Malloy, *Field Identification of Dragons*, 183).

At the present, our only information about dragon lifespan comes from Vlad.
According to Marsden, Vlad spoke of his parents in the present tense, though
Marsden could not definitely say whether that was a sure indication that they were
still alive or whether it was an indication of respect. This dragon had complete and

detailed recall of geological events of the past 4750 years for which corroborating evidence has been found and he referred to cataclysms and geologic and astronomic anomalies tentatively dated as long ago as six million years. The University of Auckland is undertaking the verification process of the information culled from the record of these conversations. In evaluating this evidence, however, it should be remembered that dragon memory is a complex process, and they do not make the same distinctions we do between what is remembered by the group and what is remembered by the individual. Certainly they are very long-lived.

It has been proposed that dragons have an extraterrestrial origin. Earth, according to this theory, is one stop on a migratory pattern that extends throughout this portion of the galaxy. Earth is seen to provide an oxygen-rich atmosphere for the young and sufficient food to support a breeding population. This theory provides answers for two problems: Why do dragons disappear for hundreds of years and return to make serious inroads in the world's food supply? And why is dragon metabolism so different from that of other creatures native to Earth? However, the theory would appear to be unnecessarily complex. Answers to these questions can be suggested by other theories that do not have to range outside of the Earth's atmosphere. The surges in apparent population can be accounted for by giving proper consideration to the size of the total dragon population, which is not large even after four breeding cycles; to the availability of land and especially ocean areas where human presence is virtually nonexistent; and to the dragon's ability to disguise himself to preserve his privacy. If the Froedlich-Marsden model for metabolic activity is taken as approximately correct, the differences between dragon digestion and that of mammals are ones of scale, rather than of kind. Even at its simplest level, metabolism is fundamentally a radical chemical change. One of the by-products of that change is heat. By taking the same basic model of the process and increasing the complexity and the scale, we arrive without serious distortion at the Froedlich-Marsden theory.

In other words, both problems answered by the extraterrestrial model can be solved or at least approached more easily by extrapolating from terrestrial phenomena. In scientific inquiry it is the custom to choose the simpler explanation over the more complex unless there is persuasive evidence to the contrary. For this reason alone, the extraterrestrial theory should not be accepted until more research is completed. There is, however, one piece of evidence that supports the extraterrestrialist position: the testimony of Vlad. In his conversations with Marsden Vlad reminisced about geological and meterological phenomena that are not part of the accepted evolution of this planet. Until his testimony can be conclusively disproved, the extraterrestrialist theory cannot be discarded altogether.

It is most likely that dragons are in fact always present in the world, even on land, but that their presence becomes evident only during the infrequent mating cycles when they make heavy demands on the human sphere. During the interim the metabolic needs of even a sizable dragon population could be met without making serious inroads into the world food supply. They live quietly, in secluded areas, at the extreme latitudes and in the sea. If they venture into more public areas, they assume the mime and travel at night. Gradually humans forget about them, as we did after the Pre-Medieval Infestation, and they recede in our common memory and become creatures of legend and myth.

Folk tradition insists that dragons are immortal. This is highly unlikely. It is true that insofar as we can ascertain on the basis of present evidence no dragon has ever died a natural death. This does not mean, however, that no dragon will ever die. They are tied to a lifespan that exceeds our understanding of that term. We do not know when the first dragons appeared, and it is extremely unlikely that we will witness the completion of the first dragon's life cycle. It is simply beyond us.

The present dramatic increase in dragon population may in fact be an indication that they are just beginning to come into prominence as an earth species.

III

EXCERPTS FROM
THE PAPERS OF MARTA FROEDLICH
AND PHILIP MARSDEN

Froedlich's Sketchbook

Very little of the total Froedlich opus is available for publication. The major portion of her work remained unpublished during her lifetime, largely because the University of São Paulo cooperated with the Brazilian government in suppressing dragon studies in the hope of discouraging dragon raids. This meant that except for a brief time between the Disaster and the onslaught of hoard fever, when the articles that have been collected for *The Anatomy and Behavior of Dragons* were written, she and her friends had to remain in Brazil and work in private. Since her death, complications between the Froedlich family and various organizations have forestalled any hopes of retrieving her work for publication.[1]

---

1 The plane crash that killed her and her companion-collaborator, Baodelio Santander, destroyed all record of her current field work. The day of the crash her family flew to São Paulo and to Cananéia and emptied the contents of her library, her study, and her apartment into cardboard boxes, which they removed to the country home of her brother near Paraná, Argentina. Her mother and her brothers had opposed her work throughout her life, just as they opposed her father's botanical studies. Señora Froedlich had resented her husband's intense interest in the plant life of Argentina and the independence it gave him. She fought with partial success to prevent his spending her family inheritance to finance field trips and to outfit his laboratory. Marta, even as a young girl, took her father's part in this struggle. From him she learned all she knew of natural sciences and techniques of observation, histology, and so forth. She accompanied him on his field trips in spite of her mother's strenuous objections. As she grew older, she lived a double life: a dutiful daughter in her mother's house, applying herself to music and needlework; and an eager apprentice in the fiercely competitive intellectual community of scientists who appreciated the zeal and ability of her amateur father. When she was nineteen, this community arranged to have her spirited away to the University of São Paulo.

Although she had had no formal education before University, her natural ability and her father's patient tutoring put her at the head of her class immediately. She completed her undergraduate and graduate work in five years. The summer after she finished her doctorate, her father died. The night of his death her mother burned his laboratory to the ground. Marta

However, among Philip Marsden's personal papers was the sketchbook Froedlich had given him when he first met her in New Haven. It is the book she filled during her first association with the dragons on the Taitao Peninsula. It was her birthday present to him shortly before she left New Haven. A few of these sketches are reproduced here for the first time.

did not return to Argentina. She supported herself throughout her life on her teaching and on the remains of a tiny trust that her father had smuggled into Brazil during the last few years of his life.

When Marta was killed at sixty-seven, her brothers and her mother, still alive and angry, were determined to have their revenge on both her and her father. However, they were prevented from destroying her work partly by pressure from the international scientific community, which sought to intercede, and more particularly by the University of São Paulo, which claimed possession of her work and had Ramon Froedlich arrested for burglary.

At this point the Latin American Coffee Growers Association cited their support of Froedlich's field work and claimed legal possession of all her papers. These they removed from the Froedlich home in Paraná and took to their headquarters in Brazil, where they were stored in a warehouse in Rio de Janeiro, still unsorted and uncatalogued in the cardboard boxes, waiting for the dispute between the Coffee Growers and the University to be settled. Fifteen years ago, when the Brazilian government nationalized the coffee industry from tree to ship, they seized possession of all related organizations as well, including the Coffee Growers. The University of São Paulo is still attempting to establish ownership of the Froedlich papers, but the litigation is enormously complex, tangled in red tape, and complicated by the suit brought against Brazil by the other nations represented in the Coffee Growers Association. Presumably the papers are still in the unmarked boxes in or near Rio.

These papers include Froedlich's complete library, her field notebooks except for those destroyed in the crash, her drawings and photographs, and the manuscript of a book that was the compilation of her lifework on dragons. She had been attempting to smuggle this work out of the country to the United States, where Academic Press had agreed to publish it.

Philip —

These are the drawings I made at my little camp at Paposo. The one of all the kits in the air is the first one I attempted. I made it my first night there. It represents what I saw when I first came over that hill and saw a dragon for the first time in my life. It was sunset and they were all out for a spin. Imagine. I thought they were huge, adults. (And I thought I had come to study geckos.)

I want you to have this book, Philip, because you will forgive the ineptitude of the person who held the pencil; and because you are today the age I was then, and because already you love these beasts as I do. Happy Birthday.

Affectionately,
Martha

THE Rsil At PLAY AT SUNSET

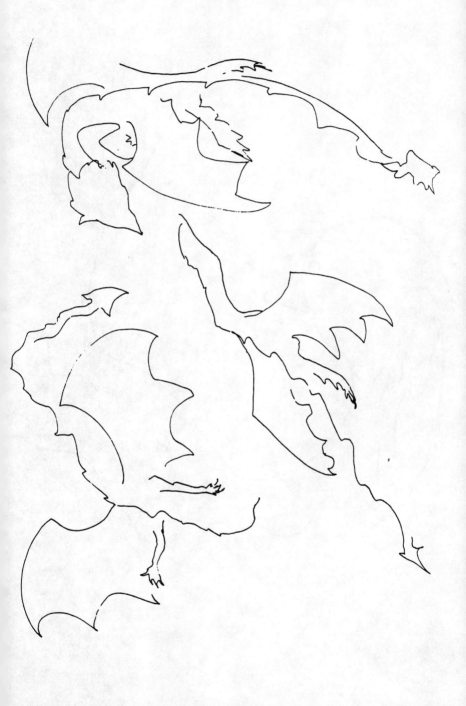

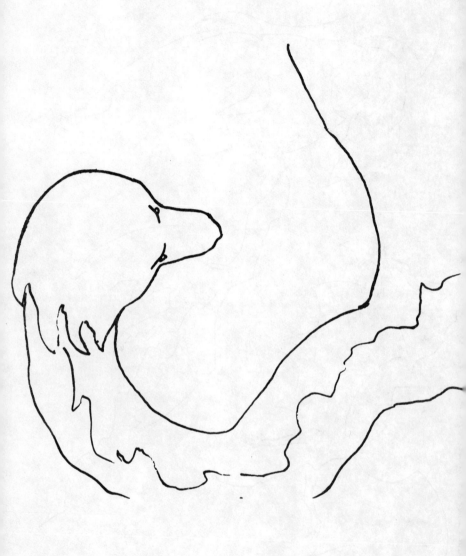

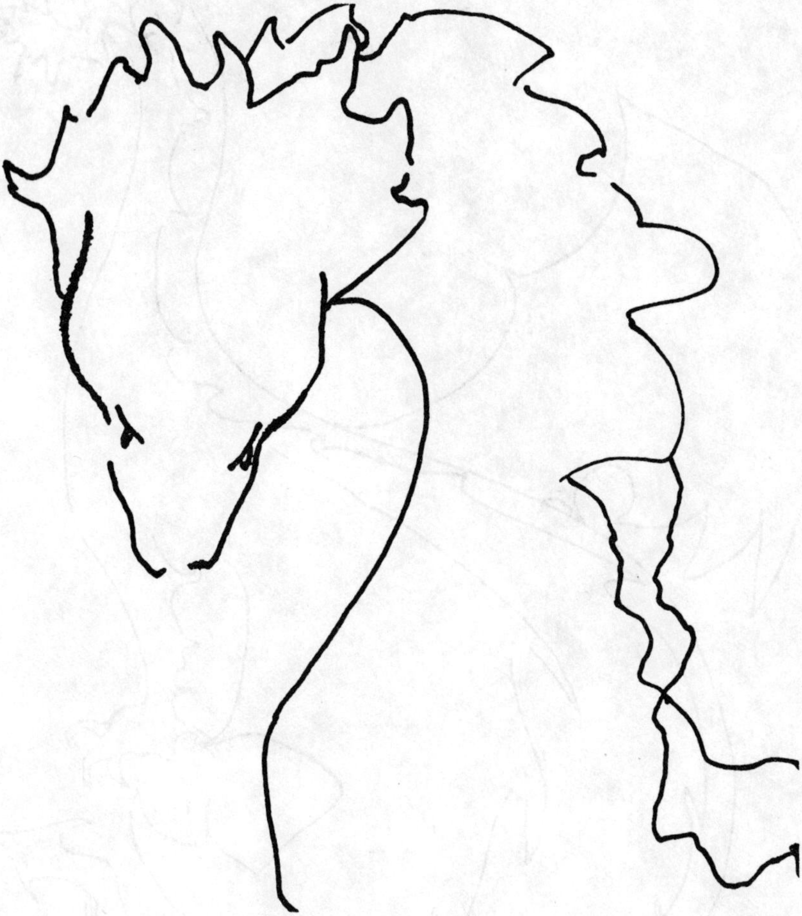

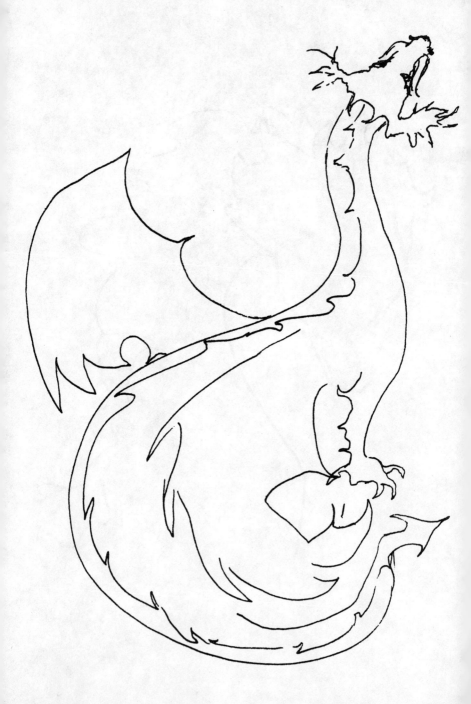

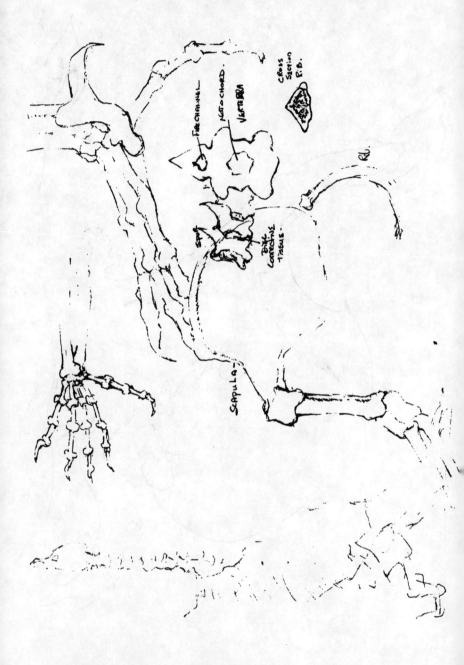

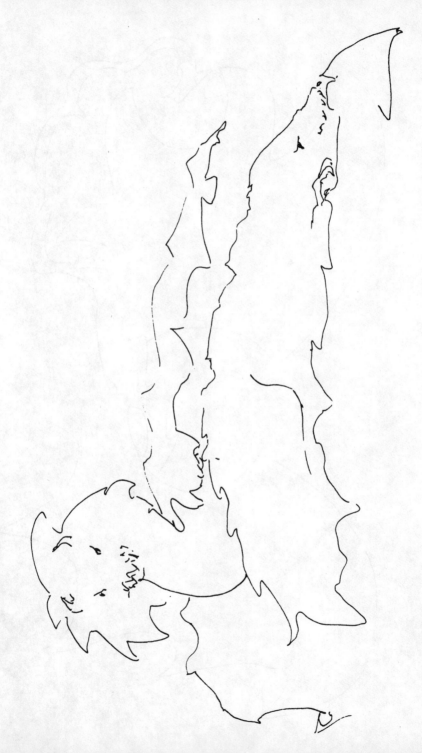

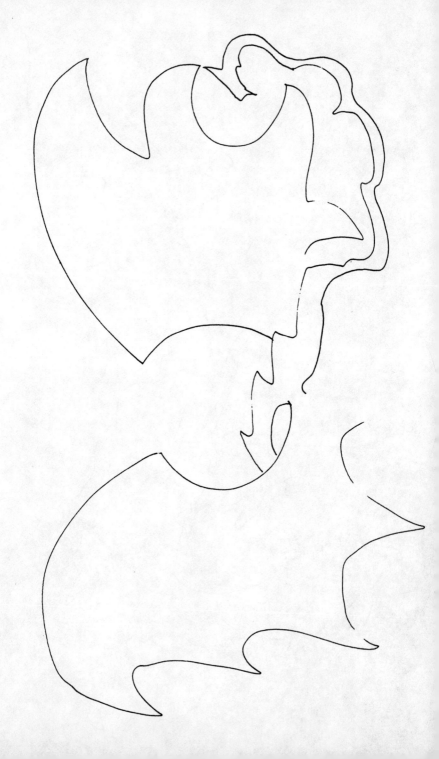

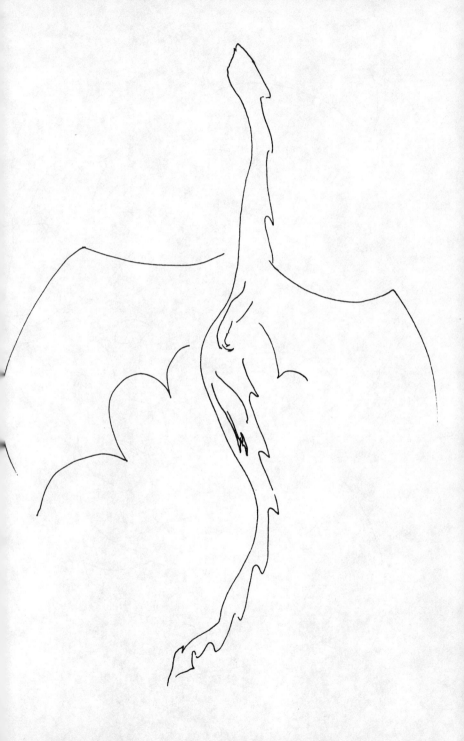

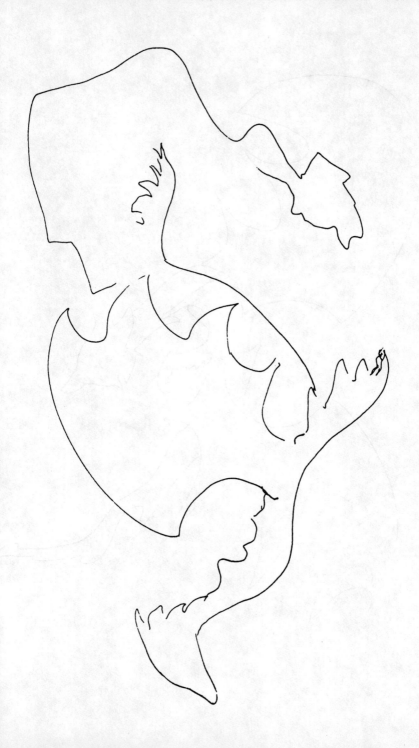

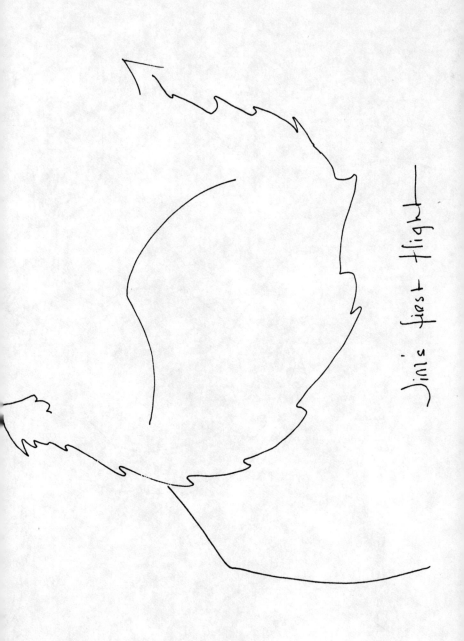

Jini's first flight

MATEO —
Waiting for me to get
up in the morning —

MATEO DISCOVERS HIS TAIL

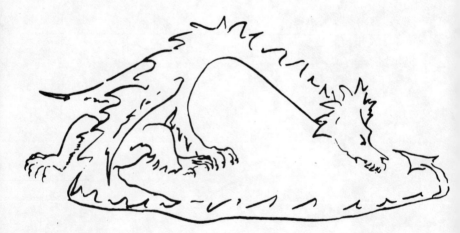

The Kit Jim Challenges the Rail over possession of a fresh kill.

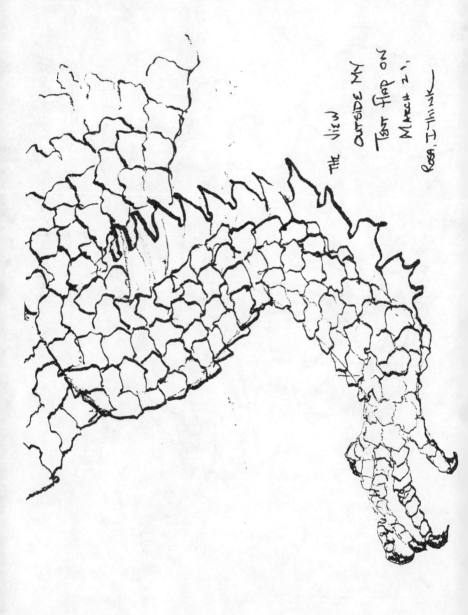

THE VIEW OUTSIDE MY TENT FLAP ON MARCH 21, Rosa, I Think

Jim preparing to pounce

Froedlich's Diary: Marsden and St. James Come to Cananéia

The following excerpts from Froedlich's diary were found among the papers in Philip Marsden's office after his death. They are used here with the permission of the literary executors of his estate. They cover a period in late September and early October while she was with Baodelio Santander in the small cottage on the coast of Brazil just north of Cananéia. This cottage was her retreat where she could work in seclusion on her dragon studies and receive dragon visitors without arousing the official displeasure of the government. This portion of the diary describes her reunion with Marsden after he left Ascension, when he came straight to Cananéia, and the inception of the association among four verminologists that has been so important for the study of dragons.

Friday, September 22. Philip arrived about 7:30 as he promised he would. Wonderful, wonderful to hug that bony frame. He looks very thin and every one of the nineteen years older since I saw him off to Ascension. He is most definitely not the young boy I met in New Haven. The dragons have taught him, and the experience has seasoned him, maybe more than he needed; there are little pain lines worn in around his temples and along the sides of his eyes, as if he'd seen a bit too much. He was genuinely relieved to be here where dragons are a matter of course. Baodelio liked him immediately. They started to shake hands, but wound up hugging each other and pounding each other on the back. It feels like a party here – that wonderful feeling of 'At last!' It's hard to tell about Philomel. She is very quiet and very observant, taking in everything with a pleased smile. Boots, jeans, grey old shirt – they must have hated her at Customs with her bag full of books and drawing materials. Just as well to be traveling with the notorious Philip Marsden. Tomorrow we'll settle down to work; right now I'm a little fuzzy in the head – too much elation.

Saturday, September 23. Got up around 4:30. No sound from the others. Spent a couple of hours writing up the wing business. Still not sure I've got the supracoracoideus right. If I'd spent more time in ornithology, maybe this would be easier for me. Took a cup of coffee out for a walk about dawn. Very few birds around. Aha, I thought, I've got a visitor. So I headed for the barranca. Philomel was there, leaning against the pine at the edge. She looked like part of the tree, really. She wasn't surprised to see me, though I was startled to find her there. I hadn't heard her leave the house. She gave me a quizzical look and nodded into the barranca. It certainly looked empty, but one sniff told me what was in there – Rosa, lovely licorice Rosa. Philomel must have sensed her there. I peered over the edge. After a while I located a large grey and red eye about three meters away. Rosa blinked when she knew I saw her. 'Doña Rosita,' I said in my best Spanish, 'this is Philomel St. James, a friend of mine. Philomel, this is Rosa.' 'I wondered what smelled so good,' said the tactful Philomel.

(Smart girl, definitely a smart girl. Anyone who can enjoy dragon stench laced with licorice is smart, obviously.) 'I am honored to meet the Doña Rosa,' continued the well-bred Philomel. Rosa, encouraged to show off, began to shed her mime, starting with her head. Philomel didn't budge, she even looked quite relaxed, though I found out later that she hadn't ever been really close to a dragon before. The dragons on Ascension had not condescended to visit her while she was there with Philip. I gather that that colony had kept its distance for the most part. Very little face-to-face contact. Anyway, there was beautiful Rosa emerging from the landscape in front of our feet. She is still quite the best-looking dragon of the bunch. Now that she is losing her silver baby dust, her blue is better than ever, more iridescent – and she always has that pleasant expression. I suppose that it is a trick of the angle of the supraorbital ridge and the curve at the corner of her mouth, but she always looks good-natured and friendly. I've never seen her angry, of course, even at Paposo, and that might change my opinion. All dragons are sinuous, but Rosa is truly graceful. She manages to make a pleasing composition out of wherever she puts herself. I could see Philomel begin to appreciate that special talent. We slid down to a comfortable sitting position and settled in for a long visit with the world's best-looking dragon. I hadn't seen her for months. Visiting with Rosa is nonverbal but very communicative some-how. She is quite friendly, really. She accepted Philomel without so much as a snort. I could almost be jealous. (Admit it, Froedlich, you are jealous.) After about thirty minutes of silent companionship Rosa came up over the edge of the barranca to brush past us on her way into the air. Dragon heat on the shoulder – lovely. She flew off slowly, but I lost her almost immediately because of her color. I could catch the glint from her wings now and then, but she herself disappeared, blue into blue.

Philomel and I walked back to the house without speaking. Philip and Baodelio were up at last, and beginning to sort through the millions of projects we hope to clear up while he is here. Nothing definite yet on how long he'll stay. Wants to redo the percussive book and work on the language itself, consolidating his Ascension work. Philomel is obviously a great help to him, quick and a steady worker. I'll try out the metabolism theory on him when things settle down a bit.

Tuesday, September 26. Rosa came back today while we were having supper outside on the veranda. She appeared suddenly over our heads – that trick of her color again. I'm sure she can't fly in mime – they just can't do that. She lay along the top of the stone wall, blocking the view of the sunset over the hill. She was curious about Philip, I could tell, though she was careful not to stare at him. She kept sniffing in his direction. Finally he couldn't take it any more and began to speak to her – directly, *in Dragon*. I was astounded! Rosa was delighted and began to glow with excitement. Philip was amused and kept watching me out of the corner of his eye. I knew he had been trying to understand Dragon, but to actually hear those sounds coming out of the mouth – and chest? – of an old friend . . . He can manage many of the sounds faultlessly. He can't get the resonance, of course, but he can make the right sounds, and Rosa was so excited she finally had to flap around to cool off. Philomel speaks a little Dragon too, apparently, and she can understand something more of what is being said. They talked a great deal of nonsense about me, apparently, he and Rosa. Philip says he hasn't the vocabulary to have a real conversation. Maybe not, but I shall learn what he knows before he gets out of here. He managed ten or fifteen minutes of what seemed very much like conversation this evening. Rosa flew off, clattering typewriter and shouting, 'Help, get off me.' It's a good thing nobody's watching this place. Five years ago the police would have been all over after that outburst.

Wednesday, September 27. I spent all that time with those dragons at Paposo and never understood a word that wasn't in Spanish, Portugese, or English. I wonder why.

Thursday, October 5. Things have settled down into a pattern now, though it is not at all the pattern I had expected when I heard that Philip was leaving Ascension and would come here to work. It's better, of course. We are all Philip's language students. Philomel is further along, since she had been working at it on Ascension. We click and groan and burble and sound terrible, but he's very patient. The other work comes along well. Baodelio has forced me to finish up the anoli stuff so we can concentrate on dragons. I mailed off the last piece to the University this morning. It is strange to go into town. I feel like a conspirator, sneaking among the innocent populace. 'Burble twiddle,' I say to the postmistress in my head. 'Good morning, Señora,' she hears, never dreaming how I am really addressing her. Baodelio and I do the shopping as usual. No use drawing attention to the fact that Philip is here. They have adjusted to one set of dragon enthusiasts finally, since no damage has come to them, but I doubt they'd be very happy to know that there were now two others around, luring the beasts into their shores. The press is preoccupied with other celebrities for the moment and leaving the half-man half-dragon alone.

Philomel has been a godsend on the anatomy. She can draw anything I describe. We all work together on the metabolism. Philip does the percussive revisions, while Baodelio and I work on the anatomy book. Philomel helps whoever needs help, but she concentrates on her drawings. Watercolor now (though she says she hates them, 'too hard') because it seems to be the best medium for dragons. It's her laugh that keeps us from getting out of sorts when we are all so tired from working all day and half the night. That and her soup.

Rosa has been back twice briefly. She tolerates all our hacking around in her beautiful liquid language with good humor. She keeps speaking

XXVIII. Froedlich and Marsden near Valentin, Chile. The southern Andes proved a difficult environment for this field population study. The team was tracked for the entire time by two dragons who remained in mime and distantly hostile. They saw few other dragons and finally counted the expedition an expensive and arduous failure. This was the only field work Froedlich and Marsden undertook together.
(*Photo: B. Santander*)

typewriter to me, though; I hate being patronized by a stupid worm. The first week of language class was murder. It has been twenty-five years since I've tried to learn anything from anyone besides myself and my reading. I couldn't make out the separate sounds. Baodelio and I practiced out loud endlessly. I just couldn't hear what I was saying. Philip made us listen to ourselves – terrible. I could hear that I was making generally the right noises. I could imitate, but it sounded like a flush to me. Yesterday, in desperation, I think, Philip threw it all over and started a different pattern, Burble Twiddle Burp Chirp, and it made perfect sense to me all of a sudden. I can't say it very well, but I understand it. Philomel gets all sounds right the first time – she just keeps quiet until she's ready, and then the first time is perfect. She and Philip have round throats. Baodelio and I have square and possibly metal ones.

Saturday, October 7. Jim came in with Rosa at dusk today. They swam ashore and lay around waiting for us to come out. It was pouring rain, which means nothing to them. They just sit there making steam and smiling. We finally gave in and joined them. Soaked in an instant. I thought at least I'd get in a burble, but not a chance. Rosa and Jim immediately got into a deep conversation. I hadn't a clue to what they were saying, and I don't think Philip did either. What it sounded like was a group of people lined up along the shore of a pond throwing in stones, big rocks, handfuls of little pebbles, and the rain droning on all the time. Occasionally I could catch a 'yes, I know you are right' kind of noise and 'are you sure that you know that I haven't observed that?' It was the wateriest conversation I've ever heard from dragons. They paid no attention to us, although it was obvious that they wanted us to be there and pay attention to them. We finally sat down on the ground and let the rain pour over us and fill in the puddles around our rear ends, while Jim and Rosa made water noises to each other. They flew off at last and we came in for hot showers. Great nerve they've got. Why don't they show off when it's dry?

Sunday, October 8. Beautiful sunrise this morning as the storm blew east. Philomel and I walked along the beach while B and P slept in as usual. Jim and Rosa were at the house when we got back, ignoring us, stretched out along the walks comfortably, just as if nothing had happened and we hadn't spent two hours in the downpour listening to them the night before. Maybe nothing did happen. Philip says that they just felt like having our company and we weren't meant to be part of the conversation. 'Just because you can echo some of the sounds doesn't mean that they want to talk with you or that they will think that you have anything to say.' Well I've always been a toy to them – I shouldn't be offended, I suppose. Philip can't be that compliant very long. I think I know now why he didn't have a lot of intimate conversations with the dragons on Ascension: better at eavesdropping than at standing around dutifully waiting for orders.

Monday, October 9. The two of them evidently mean to stick around for a while. They spent the day immobile. Rosa on the hill behind the house, and Jim stretched down the slope to the beach. His rusty, dark-green color is the perfect camouflage; he doesn't even have to get into a mime, and he disappears into the brambles and sandstone. His neck and head are in the water. He has himself positioned so that he emerges from the bushes just where the beach is narrowest. He could be a log for all the moving he does. I didn't even know he was there until the tide started to ebb and his horns began to break through the waves. By low tide he was on dry land. No motion, the tide turned and covered him up again. Gad, they are strange beasts. We have to step over Rosa to get to the path to the orchard, and clamber over Jim to get to the boats. Weird, weird, weird.

Three Letters from Marsden to Sean Jones, Introducing Vlad

The following are letters from Philip Marsden to Sean Jones. Marsden met Jones at a conference on dragon populations conducted by the Dragon Survey Group in Toronto. Jones had been especially interested in the problem of the survival of postpartum females, and had been in charge of the oceanographic survey of the Bermuda area during the Fourth Census. Marsden knew his published work and offered Jones a position at Christchurch, which he accepted.

The first letter welcomes Jones to the faculty of the School of Dragon Studies, and introduces Jones to the dragon with whom Marsden had become friendly. The second letter continues the introduction. The third letter came in answer to an enquiry from Jones about Marsden's attitude toward dragons with whom he had had conversations.

Dear Sean,

I am writing you this rather long letter because I want to ask you a favor. As you know from our conversation in Toronto, I have been lucky enough to stumble upon a good source of information. I couldn't tell you more about it, or rather him, last week as we were always in company with so many people. The conference went well, I think, but there is always such a crowd at those things it's hard to get below the surface of any subject. I am not convinced that more than a handful of them would have been particularly sympathetic to my tales of chatting with dragons, anyway. Since you are a sensible person, however, and have the right touch for this work, and can keep your own counsel, I would like to make you a party to my good luck with this source. He is a venerable beast I call Vlad, after the Impaler, which amuses him. For the past six years I have had occasional conversations with him when I can get away from school. I have kept a record of our conversations, but I am not keen to publish them or to use the information from them except in a most general way until he lets me know that he is ready to leave his island for good. You are now one of three people who know for a fact that he exists. If you agree, I will send you a copy of anything interesting that comes out of this. Philomel will have my own records. It is prudent to have two copies. One never knows. If you could just hang onto it and keep it private, I would be very grateful.

You will be coming to New Zealand sometime in the next nine months, and I will take you out to meet him if he is still in residence. It all seems a little cabalish, but there is too much to be lost by angering these beasts, as you know yourself, so I would appreciate your best silence on the whole subject. As I said, Philomel will have everything you have in the way of publishable (or worthless) material. She has my permission to publish if anything should happen to me. The permission falls on you after her. Once you get out here, we can work out a kind of rough timetable for releasing this stuff.

I admire your work on the Retirement tremendously. Precisely the kind of work that needs to be done, and you go about it in exactly the right way: lots of time in the field with the beasts themselves. You will enjoy exploring the Tasman, I think. It is quite popular as a postpartum resort, as you say, and out of the major shipping routes so you'll have more privacy than you had in Bermuda. At the School we are pretty much on our own to do as we please. We are rather an odd lot, actually. You will be our only claim to legitimate academic credentials, with all the right degrees in the right order from the right schools and the proper number of publications for your age. With you, we may be a bit more reputable in the academic world.

We will have room for seven new graduate students in the fall, and some funds for at least four of them. If you have anyone you would like to bring along, let me know. For your own work I have been able to locate a private company here in the wool business that is willing to donate for an ongoing research project. They would prefer a feeding study, but I talked them out of that. Dragons don't eat many sheep here any more, and there is plenty of work being done along the Nile by Jerez and his team. There won't be a lot of money, but there will be enough for supplies for yourself and at least one other for a field study of a couple of years. They will want a bit of reassuring from time to time that their money is producing worthwhile information. Stephansky is working on another source for you – something from the shipping area, I believe. He'll be in touch. The money problem is enough to drive me crazy. The government pays to keep the school open – half the running expenses – but we must all scratch around for the balance. Can you offer any help? I don't expect it of you, of course. University work doesn't offer many opportunities for hoarding. Ironic, isn't it, when there are dragons who could buy all the Canadian dollars in the world and barely notice the dent in their piles, and here we are scrabbling around. By the way, Mrs Bette would like to have a book list from you for the library. She will be one of the most valuable people you will know here. Send her even outrageous titles; she is very likely to find them for us.

Anyway, here is a brief account of my first encounter with Vlad just for background so you'll know a bit about it when you begin to get the stacks of fiche. It is the custom here to ignore dragons. It is considered bad form to mention them in company, and even in intimate groups; one does not discuss dragons, their whereabouts, or their practices. The loss of Stewart Island is still very much in the air. Nevertheless, word trickles into the School. Shortly after I came here from Japan, I heard that there was a solitary dragon, very large, on an island in the Tasman Sea southwest of the South Island. He was said to be hoarding, which was not very promising for my purposes since dragons are not particularly receptive to visitors while they sit on their piles. But I had not even seen a dragon for a long time, since just before my fall on Asahi-dake, and I thought about him from time to time while I waited for my body to put itself back in running order. The administrative business of setting up the School kept me occupied for the most part, and the new graduate students there could have easily taken more time than I would have had in a forty-eight-hour day. It is curious that you can be here on this smallish island, with the world's largest and most stable population of the world's largest and most spectacular beast not three hundred miles away and go for years without even seeing one in the air. They travel in and out of Stewart all the time, but I think they must move mostly by sea and at night. You never see them. The last official sighting here in Christchurch was fifty-six months ago when a small dragon passed over the northwest suburbs on his way toward Lake Colbridge. He was filmed there – a lovely violet beast streaked with green and purple. He went for a dip in the lake, snooped around a few of the 'batches' there, and then flew on south. Since then nothing.

It is a little silly to have the school here, really. If we wanted to watch them as we studied about them and wrote all our deathless prose, we'd be better off near the Faeroes. They are not a bit shy of being seen there. Before I went to Hokkaidō in my haste to fall off Asahi-dake, I spent a month in a small vessel with Emilio Branco just off the Mykines. In all there were eight days when it didn't rain. It was pretty late in the fall to be out on such a venture in the North Atlantic with only the comforts of wool clothing and the ship's heater. But we saw dragons constantly – in the air and in the sea and on the islands, and millions and millions of birds. It was a marvelous vacation. I've never seen such a variety of dragons, or so many at once. They were perfectly relaxed and didn't seem to care a bit if Emilio and I sat bundled up on the wet deck and stared at them. But they objected if we ventured too close to Mykines Sound, and they didn't care for our trying to make a pass toward Streymoy. We saw lots of whales, too, that trip. They seem to tolerate each other, whales and dragons, but the whales disappear quickly if it begins to look like mealtime. With a scope we could see the rock shores of the island strewn with vacationing worms. At night, the chanting was incessant. Sometimes we had to put out to sea to get away from it. It would rock the boat until we were afraid that she'd swamp from the rhythm. We were hallucinating, I think. The chanting would annoy the birds. If it got too loud, they'd rise off the cliffs en masse, shrilling and squawking, diving recklessly at the merrymakers. We could watch the dragons' heads rising above the tops of the cliffs as they shot warning flames to their attackers. But there is none of that holiday spirit here. Anyone foolish enough to try approaching Foveaux Strait would be incinerated on the spot. We do our dragon studies here without the distraction of having to actually see them. For all I know, there is one on my roof now, hanging his head over the gutter and staring in at the window, but I don't think so. They come to Stewart Island for dragon business, not sport. I don't know what it's like on Paramushir. The government is very touchy about even the politest inquiries, and openly hostile to any attempts to circumvent proper channels. The dragons have a very good ally there in the preservation of privacy.

Anyway, there was a dragon I knew, though hoarding, to be sure, on an island not in the protected area of Stewart Island. When the details of setting up the School began to be less overwhelming about the third year, and when the stiffness and aches from my fall began to be more nearly bearable, I began to look for a way to get out of Christchurch and into the field again. Or in this case, on the sea. It took some doing, but I finally found funding. Parliament is not keen to have people venturing out on hunts. Computer studies are more to their liking, or field work on someone else's territory. But I finally drummed up enough cash to outfit a small boat I could handle easily by myself. I put out from Milford Sound on October first with as many supplies as I could cram in. It took a long time to find him. I decided to do all the closer islands first and work my way out toward the Snares. There are a lot of bony lumps in that sea. At the end of October, on Halloween, appropriately enough, I found him. His island, one in The Snares group, is perfect for his purposes, large enough not to be too cramped, but small enough to be watched closely without much effort – and it is remote enough, Heaven knows. The wind was right, so I explored the perimeter, using my sail alone, working as close into shore as I dared in unfamiliar waters. I first spotted him festooning himself along the beach, taking the late afternoon sun. He saw me too, before I saw him. I could tell because he had begun to assume his mime, turning his tail into the colors of the rocks and making his wings look transparent, wet-sandcolored. I called out to him politely, using all the courtesies I had learned from the kits on Ascension, and saying my name very carefully.

'Oh, I know who you are,' he interrupted me in English with a heavy Kiwi accent. 'I suppose you want to converse so you can practice your sibilants.' It was very flattering to be recognized, as he well knew.

'You're a friend of what's-her-name.' He made the typewriter noise. I answered affirmatively, as politely as I could manage, and asked if he knew her. No, he didn't, but he heard about her here and there. It didn't matter too much what he was saying; I was busy mastering my adrenalin. Every hair on my body was perpendicular to my skin. I'd seen hundreds of dragons before and been closer to scores of them than I was to this one, but there is something rather overwhelming about Vlad. He is bigger than any other dragon I've been able to observe closely, and he has a presence that is unmistakable. He doesn't really mime very well; you always feel that there is something tremendous and awake in the vicinity. Even now, after I have known him for several years and have spent many weeks with him, I am always a bit unnerved in his company.

There is another reason it didn't matter too much what he was saying: dragons are – well, indirect in conversation. They will say what pleases them for the occasion, regardless of how it fits with what they know to be true. I knew that he could just as easily be one of the dragons Marta knew on Taitao as he could be a total stranger to her. But at least he wasn't finishing off his mime and hadn't bothered to belch at me. I took heart and sat quietly in the boat. He resumed his Observation, staring unblinking in all directions at once, the way they do. So I took in the sail, let out the anchor, and just sat too, watching him and trying to memorize the island. We watched the sunset, rather glorious over the sea that evening.

I can't begin to count the hours I have sat, or stood, quietly in the presence of some dragon or another. I've gotten used to having three-quarters of my body asleep. I rather enjoy the whole process by now. It's good for me, I think, just to be still and stay awake. I'm impatient by nature. I wouldn't want to doze off in those situations. I did that once on Ascension. I was sitting on a kind of rock seat that had been warming in the sun all morning. There was a lovely curve, just right to rest my back. I was watching a couple of kits practice stealing each other's hoards. They switched to knotting and fell to napping and before I knew it I was aware of being very hot on the feet and woke with a start to find Giselle, an adult aunt, asleep with her belly on my toes. I stayed awake after that. She could have eaten me without having to take two bites. She preferred fillets, though, I remembered that night.

After the sun was thoroughly down and the breeze was beginning to pick up for the evening, I began to wonder what I would do for the night. I knew I could stay in the boat, but I was not sure that I could stay awake, and I wasn't about to trust him either to stick around for me to get forty winks, or to curb his appetite in the presence of such a convenient, if tough, meal. 'You could be putting your boat up 'n here,' he said suddenly, indicating a sloping shelf with his tail. 'An' I couldn't get at you if you was to sleep in 'at little crack. The wind'll be setting up pretty good here in 'n hour or so.' It was an excellent southern Pennsylvania Mountain accent this time. Did he know I was from outside Harrisburg? He is inordinately fond of his collection of accents, proud even for a dragon. During the next three days he showed them all off to me. Or at least I heard hundreds of variations on English pronunciation. As time wore on he used them less frequently. He accommodates me by speaking simple Dragon most of the time, but even now he'll occasionally remember a particularly choice bit of slang he'd picked up somewhere and trot it out to show it off. Judging from the number and the accuracy, I would have to guess that he has spent time in every English-speaking country, and in all the major regions of each one. He knows quite a bit of street Portugese from Rio too, and can do a hilarious recital of a soccer match crowd after Flavio Jibáro has been red-carded.

The narrow cleft he had chosen for me that night was quite dry and roomy enough for me to stretch out in. Discretion advised me to follow his polite suggestion. I pulled the boat up and stretched out, trying to look relaxed, but fighting to stay awake.

Finally I decided, what the hell, and went off to sleep. In the morning he was gone. By the time I'd made a fire and had some coffee, though, he dangled a foot over the edge of the cliff that rimmed the beach. Sort of an offhand way of saying, 'I'm coming and I don't want to scare you out of your tiny wits.' But then he ruined it all by falling over the edge all at once. Couldn't resist the temptation. He thought it was a tremendous joke and stamped around for hours congratulating himself on having unnerved me for the day. Broke the mast of the boat too, though that might not have been an accident. He kept asking me how quickly I could get it fixed. The truth of the matter was, I think, he was just getting over that siege of hoarding and was ready for any distraction. I looked like too good a prospect for weeks of amusement. He wasn't about to let me get away before I'd admired him as much as he thought proper. He helped me poke up my fire (dragons are just the thing if your wood's wet) and caught a lovely bass for my breakfast.

He kept after me that day, asking me where was I going to sleep now, still in that tiny crack? He examined my sleeping bag, being careful not to touch it too long, so it wouldn't melt. 'You'll need a bit of shelter if it starts to rain.' 'You could take your sail, now, no good since the stick broke, and lay it across the top of the crack. This rock will hold this corner down in a wind.' 'If you would move your boat up here, the highest tide wouldn't bother it and it would be out of the way.' He made it clear that I was not free to leave the beach. The cliff marked the edge of my exercise yard. He trusted me to swim, though. 'Very good for the body, swimming,' in a strong Cockney. He was an interesting companion. Lots of variety, you might say, and always that realization that at any turn of a whim he could extinguish me in an instant.

After a few days, though, he didn't care much what I did. He even helped me find a replacement for my mast. I didn't see him constantly.

He would swim off or fly away. Sometimes he would disguise himself
and wait to see what I would do when he wasn't around. But that proved
to be too much like what I was doing when he was around, and he got
tired of it. Often he would lie along the edge of the cliff and stare. I knew
not to interrupt him when he was doing that. I worked on my notes. He
was right about swimming. I swam several times a day, and I could feel
the improvement in my bones. I finished recovering from the fall there,
and now I only have a couple of reminders, in joints that don't flex all the
way. I spent the whole summer on that island and stayed on into the fall.
By the end of June, though, I'd used up all the time I could take away
from my other life. I got ready to go and pushed off. He watched me leave
and sent a burst of flame after me.

Since that first summer I have been back many times. Sometimes he is
there and sometimes he isn't. It doesn't matter really. I've taken Philomel
with me, and they get along well enough. He enjoys her, I think – the
feminine touch. And she is sturdy enough to take him without flinching.
I will be glad for you to meet him too. Philomel will be able to help you
with your Dragon when you get here. Between us we'll get you fluent
enough to impress the old beast.

Let me know when the first packet of fiche arrives. The mail off these
islands is reliable enough, but sometimes takes a while.

P.

Dear Sean,
I gather from your work, and our conversations in Toronto that you know
a few words of Dragon, but that you haven't talked with the beast himself.
There is little in the climate of the DSG to encourage interspecies
communication, certainly, and I suppose that all the floating about off
Bermuda that you did was strictly Observation. Usually people who know
a bit of Dragon transliterated (and there are few enough of them) cannot
make out spoken Dragon when it is spoken by the genuine article. I am
enclosing a recording of Vlad's voice, speaking Dragon on a simple level
– mine. If you play it over and over, you will get used to the sound and
be able to pick out individual words. If you are indeed going to join us
here, you might as well get started on the language process. Perhaps your
Dragon is better than I think, in which case I apologize (and am delighted).
Let me know how you come along with this sample. He is scolding me
for not coming to see him in July (which shows how much he knows about
academic life, and what a realistic idea he has about human endurance in
the winter alone at sea in a very small boat). After the bits I mumble, he
goes on about friends he had once. He is never specific about dates. He
is describing the chanting they were doing. I purposely sent you this rather
unusual sound to steady your nerves for the visit I plan for you after you
get here. The last three or four minutes are where he is agreeing to meet
you. Thought you'd like that. I left in the description I gave him of you

so you'll know how to act. Don't worry about not being fluent. There aren't a handful of people who know twenty phrases. We train our students here, but only one out of three really gets the hang of it. Philomel is far and away the best. She'll see to it that you get all that you can stand once you settle in.

I will be going back out to The Snares in a couple of weeks when the school year closes down, so this will be the last shipment for a while. I should have some more for you when I get back in six weeks or so. If Vlad is feeling chatty, I may stay longer. I fear he may be getting cabin fever, though; he's been on that island for a long time, and the hoard doesn't really interest him any more. One day I'll sail out there and find it empty. Not this time, I hope. The weather service thinks he's still in residence.

Sorry you have had to take some officious disapproval from the DSG for your move to NZ. There doesn't seem to be a way to reconcile the speakers and nonspeakers at the moment. Philomel says they don't want to believe that a mere beast could think. She calls them the 'crown of creation crowd.' Once you get down here, you can read their publications and correspond with the ones who matter and forget the rest.

P.

Dear Sean,

As you see, more fiche after all. One last shipment before I set out. I assume that the U of T has audiovisual display for these things. In answer to your question, no, I have not always liked every dragon I met. Vlad is far and away the best, though I will always be very fond of Rosa and Jim in a way that is quite particular to them. Marta somehow attracted the best qualities in the dragons (and people) she knew. She loved all the beasts she was associated with – partly because she was very tolerant herself and was never anything less than delighted by their variety and self-possession. Partly, too, because she had the wits and composure to fit into that initial encounter with them and retained the sense of wonder it gave her. She was always quiet, respectful, charmed by their presence – maybe because she couldn't understand what they were saying. Even after she got the knack of the fundamentals of Dragon, she was never fluent at all. Nor was Santander. Dragons adored her, though, and by extension, Santander. They simply loved having Marta and Baodelio around. Marta and Baodelio did not try to converse with their keepers. They worked very hard at learning to understand what was being said, but the beasts don't really talk much of the time anyway, only the kits babble on and on and on. . . . It was a kind of easy, relaxed companionship. The dragons gave no thought to how their pleasure might discomfit their pet humans. They were never harmed, of course, but I remember one week there at Cananéia when Philomel and I were frantic with worry. Marta and Baodelio had gone out for a walk one evening and were followed by Jim, who had been hanging around the house. Just after sunset we saw them out in the boat with Jim swimming around them and making Knots over their heads. We knew that Jim wouldn't hurt them or drown them purposely, but Jim is a large animal and the boat was very small. We didn't see them again for six days. They showed up one afternoon, laughing lightly, quite unconcerned. Jim had taken them off for a long boat ride and then escorted them ashore in some forsaken place. Rosa had joined them, and Marta and Baodelio were allowed to spend five days cooling their heels while their hosts engaged in Observation. There was enough to eat in the area, so they didn't starve. They hadn't minded it a bit, in fact. To them, it was all part of being interested in dragons. In Paposo, on the second trip, they had been befriended, in a more civilized way, by a roil, but none of those was a regular visitor at Cananéia. Occasionally one would drop by, or another stray out looking around, but Rosa and Jim were the only regulars. Because of their association with Marta and Baodelio, Jim and especially Rosa were sweet – which is not a word I would apply to many dragons.

My own relations with dragons have been more complex. After my initial introduction to Jim in New Haven, I concentrated on learning how to communicate with them on a rational level, and I have paid the price in complexity, as is fitting. I did not talk to the dragons on Ascension. Before the base was destroyed, I did not have the skill, and after that experience I somehow couldn't bring myself to address them. It seemed disrespectful somehow to the people who had lived on that island before the beasts chose to wipe them out. When Philomel came, I had a fair vocabulary. I had practised hours upon endless hours learning to make the sounds and form the syllables. She is a very quick study, as you will see, and we were able to listen to the colony and then to each other, and I learned more. But it was Rosa who made me overcome my reticence. There was a little low stone wall around the veranda at Marta's home on the coast. Rosa came and lay along that wall one evening while we were having supper. She is a very beautiful dragon and has a friendly, open expression. She is small too, given the breed. That evening she was very curious about me. I was new to the group – Marta and Baodelio were old pals, and she'd met and liked Philomel that morning. But I was a puzzle to her. I hadn't been subjected to the aggressive curiosity of an adult dragon before. I could feel her bending her will on me, prying. So I spoke to her – much to Marta's surprise and Philomel's delight. After overcoming that hurdle, I've spoken with many dragons, maybe as many as thirty different dragons in Hokkaidō, in the Sudan, in Sichuan Province, even in Uzbekistan. Most of those were business talks. 'Look here, excuse me, but if you continue to eat these animals, the food supply for all these people will be completely wiped out and they won't be able to raise any more nice horses and camels for you.' 'Pardon me for interrupting your observations, but the people who live here are going to be building a road through this area and it may prove to be disturbing to you. When will it be convenient for them to start the blasting? They would prefer not to inconvenience you in any way.' That, of course, was the literal truth. That conversation, or rather address, I aimed in the direction of an ugly, ill-tempered red worm napping – not observing – on the seacoast of Ireland near Errigal. He was, I think, quite vile: incinerating anything that happened to get in his line of vision, killing off things that annoyed him, like the children from a neighboring farm who were too noisy one afternoon. Didn't eat them either. Just, me first and to hell with the rest of you. The road project had been held up for eighteen months while he took his naps and made a murdering pest of himself. He flew off without the courtesy of an answer. For the most part dragons are civil, uncomplaining, ready to live and let live. They are quite self-absorbed, or absorbed with each other, at any rate. You can be a week in their presence and they won't acknowledge your existence. Though they must have heard me practicing their language, they never said a word to me on Ascension – and they knew me pretty well after eighteen or nineteen years. I sometimes wonder why I bother with them, but that is only when I'm not around them. I've never been even faintly bored in their presence. They are extraordinarily beautiful to watch, and there is a soothing completeness in their motions and general being that never dulls. If you are interested in them at all, they are endlessly interesting. But I can't say that I've really liked more than a handful of them or been fond of more than four. Vlad is the only dragon who has been willing to give me consideration and respect – mutuality – and my only real conversations have been with him. Vlad is different, of course. Humans are his hobby, and I think my stubborn interest in a beast that has given me so much pain awoke a kind of fellow feeling in him.

P.

Conversation between Marsden and Vlad

Dear Sean,

I have had an extraordinary conversation with Vlad – almost a glimpse of what it must be to think like a dragon. It was short, only one long evening, and like no other conversation I've ever had with him, much less with any other dragon. I'm afraid that it will turn out to be a kind of farewell gesture. He left the island during the night after this talk, and had not returned by the time I had to leave. He's gone off for short trips before, so maybe this was not my last visit with him, but time is running fast now, and I'm uneasy.

Usually our conversations, though cordial, consist of my asking him questions and his correcting my Dragon, ignoring my inquiry and asking me questions about some human quirk or habit. I don't know what got into him, that he talked about himself. He has described places he's been, things he's seen, sometimes even other dragons, like his first mate, but he is always absent from his descriptions. Usually dragons aren't even mentioned. This is about as close as he gets to biography: 'You should have seen this place when I first came here. Birds and debris. There was hardly room to get the stuff into the cave.' The 'stuff' in this case was, I presume, the first shipment of his loot. Or 'I never had to say one word to her or she to me. We had to talk to the kits, of course.' When he feels garrulous, he usually expatiates on the particular delights of some gustatory treat. Some of those descriptions I could do without. But he doesn't talk much, ever. That evening, for some reason, he started talking about knotting with his siblings. Knotting talk always goes past me. They have terms for speed, relationship, altitude, sequence of attitude . . . hundreds of terms, none of which I recognize and none of which he has ever condescended to translate or explain. But that night, talking about knotting with his siblings, he seemed more open than usual. When he lapsed into a long silence I asked him, 'But after you left the cache, what did you do then?'

'It was the Wandering.'

'Could you explain wandering?'

'Not wandering, human, the Wandering.' He sank into the remote condition that meant that he was conversing with himself on dragon terms, on a level from which I was thoroughly excluded. Not hostile, simply remote – as if I were a stone or a twig – a non-interactor. After five minutes or so he resurfaced. His eyes regarded me with that air of mischief and affection that I have always found so hard to deal with. 'I will talk to you in your own language, since it is all so much easier for you if we limit ourselves that way. After I left my father – he bellowed and flamed for us as we flew off – and my siblings, I did what dragons do when they are not mating, as you so indelicately call it, and when they are free from the terror of the hoard. Don't raise your eyebrows, small human, it is indeed a terror to be hoarding. I suppose you will ask me about that too one day. The times when I have been compelled to hoard . . .' He cupped his collar forward and raised his scales slightly before he resumed. 'A dragon is alone, still and complete in the Wandering. The first Wandering is not as good as the later ones. I learned how to Wander fully only after years of practice.'

Hardly believing my good luck at finding him so chatty, I risked another direct question. 'But what is it like? Why do you do that?'

He hardly seemed to notice me. I could only see a portion of his head. His long grey-green body stretched away from the fire and disappeared in the dusk. I could almost have been alone on that rocky beach.

'I am absolutely content in the Wandering. I take the food I need wherever I choose. I observe. I record. I remember. I am aware. You could not understand it, Philip, even you. You do not have the words to string together to make the right sense to approximate it.' He paused. 'Do you know what this means?' He pronounced a Dragon word I had heard from Jim, and two times on Ascension, but which I had never been able to identify. Nor had I been able to ask about it, since most of the sounds were ones that I could not reproduce. 'It describes the Wandering. In your tiny vocabulary it seems something like . . . "he is, he is not unlike." It doesn't scale down to your size too well. The Wandering is a very good time for a dragon.' His voice took on an added timbre. 'It is when I feel the most dragon.'

'You say a dragon is alone in the Wandering. Do you avoid each other?'

'No. But we do not seek each other out. We do not need company. Of course, "alone" is not accurate either. It might be better to try "he is solitary and rooted in dragons." We remain aware of each other, as we are aware of other phenomena. Now that is a good word, "phenomena." It sounds fine, and it is good to pronounce.' He practiced saying it several ways: gurgling it, squeaking it, rolling it out, augmented with the bellow-chamber resonance. 'It is a witty word, too: complicated sound for a complex idea, but one is longer than more-than-one. Phenomenon. Quite a satisfactory word. The trouble with your language, Philip, with all your human languages, is that you can only say one thing at once, one thing pronounced laboriously, carrying a very imprecise aura of associations. And a very inexact receiving apparatus inside the silly little flaps of gristle too, I might add. If you could use Dragon properly, we could talk about "phenomena" now and the Wandering at the same time, and we could comment on how the two resonate together, simultaneously as we talked, and we could watch and comment on our surroundings percussively. But you do one thing at a time, because your language is confined to that, and you do not have the body skills to articulate the other things you are thinking while you are forming words and sentences.' Suddenly he grabbed my left leg and shook it gently (for him). 'There, it will wake up more quickly now. If you will put more weight here' – he touched my right hip – 'your leg will not go numb like that while you sit so still. In a way that is why I like to talk with you, Philip. It is like trying to fly with one wing – not very efficient, but good exercise. While I'm alone, I'm aware of other dragons. If a Chant is forming, I always go to it, for instance, or occasionally to a Knot. And sometimes I like to have my what you call "observation place" near those of other dragons. It's convenient for hunting. But during the Wandering – I don't need anything.' He rocked at me kindly and chuckled.

'You like the Wandering, then, quite a bit.'

'I relish it.' He has a way of saying 'relish' that gives me the impression he is licking his chops. The hairs on my arms are always alarmed. He shifted around on the sand. I could hear him refolding his wings.

'Why do you stop Wandering then?'

'Because of the other hungers, hoarding and the cache.'

'Do you just decide to start hoarding, or to have kits? How do you choose which to do?'

There was a long silence then. The last of the evening light faded, the breeze shifted to the north. I put more wood on the fire, sure that I had lost him. It was, by then, the longest conversation I had had with him since the first time on the island. I reviewed it carefully, so that I could write it down accurately later. I put on a bigger log. I could see his eye and the glint of the light on his scales. He rocked at me amiably.

'Choose, no, Philip. But I can tell when the hungers begin. They increase bit by bit over the years of Wandering. I begin to spend more time remembering than I did at the beginning. If I remember my own cache or my other nestings – "remember," "remember" is not the right word, small human, but we will say "remember" – when I begin to remember nestings more strongly than I remember other things, then I know that one day when the Wandering is over, I will be nesting again myself. Ah, but if I begin to remember the things I have experienced in the long past, the eloquent land shapes, the details of the leaves, the little creatures and the great beasts that cannot be any longer, when I begin to be aware with my remembering and with my present senses . . . Do you know what it is like for us to remember, Philip? It is as if we were present again – as if it were happening for the first time, but commented upon simultaneously. Not like your dreaming, if I understand correctly what you try to explain to me – when we remember, we are fully present in the experience and our bodies are not inert, though they are often motionless, and all our faculties are ours to use. If I understand your dreaming, you cannot write or do counting while you dream. If you try to interpret the little marks in your books in your dream, you cannot do it; you cannot even see them properly. But we are not limited that way in our remembering, and neither are we cut off from the present world while we are remembering. We remain aware while we remember. When I begin to remember the tiny creatures I have experienced, and the shapes the stars used to make in the long night sky, when I begin to remember them, and know that they are present only in my remembering, and that they will never be again, and that all that I observe now will also change and fade and cease to be – that only dragons remember and that they must witness it all – then the hoard hunger begins to grow, and the bitterness and the salt bleak, and I know that this Wandering is precious and will not last much longer, and that when I come from it, I will be in the grip of the hoard and imprisoned for long, narrow years to come. Ah, Philip, to be free from the hoard. You have much we can envy in your brief lives and small visions.'

He receded again, but I spoke anyway, in Dragon – anything to draw him out again. 'But the hunger for the cache brings you joy?'

'I will not talk to you about nesting, Philip. You know enough of human kits to understand that.'

He slid into the water and disappeared. But later that night I woke to see him out over the ocean, all incandescent, knotting and soaring alone in the night sky, his fire reflected in the sea.

P.

Suggestions for Further Reading

The basic resource for information on all aspects of dragon studies is the *Journal of Verminology*, published by the New Zealand School of Dragon Studies, which includes a current bibliography in each number. All of Froedlich and Marsden's works are included in their annual Comprehensive Bibliography in March. The *Proceedings* of the 58th and 59th International Congress of Anatomists include papers on various dragon studies.

Occasionally the New Zealand School of Dragon Studies publishes Working Papers by faculty and graduate students in Christchurch. These are usually on language or behavior. The introductory material Marsden prepared for his second edition of the *Lexicon of the Percussive Language of Dragons* (Brill) is excellent. Unfortunately this little book is out of print and not readily available. Aspects of dragon behavior can be explored more fully in publications from the Sudan and from China, though for the most part the latter are translated into only Spanish or German. Stephen Lucan's exciting account of *The Destruction of San Cristóbal* is not a scientific book, but is informative in a popular vein. Similarly LeGuin's work from the East and West Reaches may be read with profit.

More comprehensive treatment of the general biology of dragons is found in the Froedlich-Marsden articles in *Anatomista Latinoamericano*. These articles have been collected into a single volume, *The Anatomy and Behavior of Dragons*, which is available in several editions and in translation: English, Spanish, German, Chinese, and French. The best edition is probably the one prepared by Sean Jones for Addison-Wesley, as it includes numerous plates. This fundamental work may be supplemented by Emilio Branco's contributions to the *Revista Zoológica* and by various publications of Wilhelm Steinmetz, Wanda Grenner, and Serafin Del Rio. The publications of the University of São Paulo included several articles by Froedlich and her associates before the Official Toleration Act. These are available only in Portuguese.

Bibliography of Works Cited

Academia Sinica. *Long Yanjiu.* 6, 11. Beijing, China.

Branco, Emilio. 'Classification of Dragons into One Species Using Physical Appearance as the Primary Criterion', *Zoological Journal* XIV. Chicago, Illinois, USA.

———. 'Delegaciónes a los dragones en Paraguai'. *Boletin de Estudios Cientificos*, Instituto por las Ciencias Naturales. Numero 7, Ascunción, Paraguay.

———. 'Dragon Flight', *Flight* No. 7:30, 21–22, Houston, Texas, USA.

———. 'Estimación de los tamanos y los pesos dragones maduros: unos metodos especificos'. *Revista Zoológica* 10, 89–94. Basel, Switzerland.

Branco, Emilio, and Baodelio Santander. 'Delegaciones a los dragones', Boletin de Estudios Cientificos: *Publicaciones del Institute de San Martin de la Playa*, numero 6. Buenos Aires, Argentina.

Bronowski, Jacob. *The Ascent of Man.* Little Brown, 1973, Boston, Massachusetts, USA.

Bruford, David W. *The Golden Dragon and the Meaning of Life*, Seaward Press. San Francisco, California, USA.

Canada. *RCMP Advisory Bulletin* 431J XP 117. 'Instructions for Sighting the X12R on a Superheated Target'. Ottawa, Ontario, Canada.

Canadian Photographer, No. 3. Vancouver, British Columbia, Canada.

Del Rio, Serafin. See Wanda Grenner.

Dragon Survey Group. United States-Canadian Publications. #DCXB 3499431–DCXB 3499784. #34 JWB10–9:60 to 10:28. US-Canadian Federal Publications Office, Calgary, Alberta, Canada.

DuForêt, Claude. 'Evidence du "feu-dragon" manifestée par la technique de thermographie de Grenet: premiéres données experimentales', *Proceedings of the Fifty-eighth International Congress of Anatomists, Paris.* International Congress of Anatomists, Le Havre, France.

Froedlich, Marta. *Anatomy and Behavior of Dragons.* Edited by Sean Jones (trans. of *A anatomia e comportamento dos dragões*). Addison-Wesley Press, New York, USA.

Fuentes, Hernanda del, and Carmino Garcia Puebles-Gil. 'Los dragones evitaron Hispanoamerica'. *Revista Chileno de los ciencias naturales y sociologias: los trabajos a la Universidad de Santiago de Chili.* Universidad de Santiago, Santiago, Chili.

Glaumer, Frederick J. *The Basic Book of Unusual Beasts.* Chatto and Windus, London, England.

Green Wilderness Society: The Northwest Rescue Committee. *Report Number One.* Green Wilderness Society, Edmonton, Alberta, Canada.

Grenner, Wanda, and Serafin Del Rio. 'Uno descripción de la nacimiento de ocho dragones infantes: Rio Neuquén, Argentin'. *Anatomista Latinoamericano: Archivos del Institut de Estudios Anatomilogicos Alejandro Robles-Maldonado* XII:8. Asunción, Paraguay.

———. 'Infant Development of Dragon Kits'. *Revista Zoológica*, 14:7, Basel, Switzerland.

———. 'Pre-mating Behavior of Two Dragons Selecting a Cache Site on the River

Neuquén in the Argentine Highlands'. *Zoological Journal* IX. University of Chicago, Chicago, Illinois, USA.

Halib, Mustafa, and Virginia Wali. 'The Cache on Al-Bahr-al-Ghazal'. *Dragon, Non-Dragon Interface: Occasional Papers*, 3. University of Khartoum, Khartoum, Sudan.

Hansen, Chlorenda B. 'Computer Analysis of Dragon Chants, Masaji Nos. 14, 83, 107, 212'. Dissertation. Massachusetts Institute of Technology. Cambridge, Massachusetts, USA.

Harada Gorô. 'Kirensk', *Nagata Hōkoku* #23. Nagata Foundation, Kyōto, Japan.

———. 'Ryū no Chikuzai no Kaisetsu'. (Profile of a Hoarding Dragon), *Nagata Zaidan no Kiroku* #9. Nagata Foundation, Kyōto, Japan.

———. 'Taibaishan', *Nagata Hōkoku* #83. Nagata Foundation. Kyōto, Japan.

Hashima Masaharu with Anthony Taylor. *The Treasure of Nagata*. Macmillan Co., New York, USA.

Hayashiya Shin'ichi. *Nagata Hokōku* #33. Nagata Foundation, Kyōto, Japan.

Houbek, Thomas Carleson. *Verminous Depletion of Marine Fauna*. Pacific Winds Press. Santa Barbara, California, USA.

Jones, Sean. 'Assumption and Maintenance of the Mime in the Open Sea'. *New Zealand School of Dragon Studies Working Paper 20*. New Zealand School of Dragon Studies, Christchurch, New Zealand.

———. 'Dragons in the Sargasso Sea: Feeding Behavior'. *Canadian Science Newsletter* 57:42. University of Saskatchewan, Saskatoon, Saskatchewan, Canada.

———. 'Female Dragons over the Bermuda Rise: Population Variations over a Twenty-Five-Year Period'. *US-Canadian Dragonographic Publication No. 47*. United States-Canadian Dragon Survey Group Publications. Calgary, Alberta, Canada.

———. 'Females in the Tasman Sea: Preliminary Report'. *New Zealand School of Dragon Studies Working Paper 15*. New Zealand School of Dragon Studies, Christchurch, New Zealand.

———. 'The Three Stages of Retirement'. *New Zealand School of Dragon Studies Working Paper 12*. New Zealand School of Dragon Studies, Christchurch, New Zealand.

Khartoum, University of. *Dragon, Non-Dragon Interface*. University of Khartoum, Khartoum, Sudan.

Liu Li-chou. 'Late Adolescence in Dragons'. *American Journal of Comparative Biology*, Vol. 23, No. 7. Published by the Society for the Study of Comparative Biology, Oklahoma City, Oklahoma, USA.

Lucan, Stephen. *The Destruction of San Cristóbal*. McClelland and Stewart, Toronto, Ontario, Canada.

McAlister, Ferdinand. 'Location of Dragon Observation Sites in Orogenically Significant Zones'. Dissertation. University of Auckland, Auckland, New Zealand.

McArdle, Antonia. 'A Reinterpretation'. *Zoological Review 28:2*. Royal Institute for the Natural Sciences, Oxford, England.

Malloy, Lewellen, and Stanley Rubson. *Field Identification of Dragons*. University of Minnesota Press, Minneapolis, Minnesota, USA.

Marsden, Philip. 'Dissolution of the First Roil on Ascension'. *New Zealand School of Dragon Studies Working Paper 18*. New Zealand School of Dragon Studies, Christchurch, New Zealand.

———. 'Evidence of Affection in the Cache'. *New Zealand School of Dragon Studies*

Working Paper 8. New Zealand School of Dragon Studies, Christchurch, New Zealand.

———. 'Knotting Displays of Kits and Adults on the Taitao Peninsula, reported by Froedlich and Santander'. *New Zealand School of Dragon Studies Working Paper 3*. New Zealand School of Dragon Studies, Christchurch, New Zealand.

———. *Lexicon of the Percussive Language of Dragons*. Brill, Leiden, Netherlands.

———. 'Some Thoughts on Dragon Apprehension and Appreciation of Human Arts'. *New Zealand School of Dragon Studies Working Paper 6*. New Zealand School of Dragon Studies, Christchurch, New Zealand.

———. 'The Undetected Presence of Dragons in Metropolitan Centers'. *New Zealand School of Dragon Studies Working Paper 9*. New Zealand School of Dragon Studies, Christchurch, New Zealand.

Del Rio, Serafin. See Wanda Grenner.

Rubsen, Stanley. See Lewellen Malloy.

St. James, Philomel. 'Classification of Percussive Sound'. *New Zealand School of Dragon Studies Working Paper 4*. New Zealand School of Dragon Studies, Christchurch, New Zealand.

Santander, Baodelio. 'The Sustenance of Young Dragons'. *Proceedings of the Fifty-eighth International Congress of Anatomists, Rome*. Published by the International Congress of Anatomists, Le Havre, France.

———. 'Comparison of the Andreanof Knot and the Bach Passacaglia and Fugue in D minor'. *New Zealand School of Dragon Studies Working Paper 23*. New Zealand School of Dragon Studies, Christchurch, New Zealand.

———. 'Mating Display: Andreanof Island', *New Zealand School of Dragon Studies Working Paper 7*. New Zealand School of Dragon Studies, Christchurch, New Zealand.

Shigehara Yukio. 'Ryū no Chikuzai no Hitotsu no Riyū no Kenkyū'. (An exploratory study of a possible reason for hoarding). *Nagata Zaidan no Kiroku #20*. Nagata Foundation, Kyōto, Japan.

Steinmetz, Helmut. 'Gathering Data on Dragons: The Problem of Duration'. *Proceedings of the Fifty-ninth International Congress of Anatomists, Paris*. Published by the International Congress of Anatomists, Le Havre, France.

———. 'Influence of Heat on the Pre-natal Kit'. *Journal of Comparative Anatomy CLVI no. 4*. Clarence and Julia Beade Foundation. Tucson, Arizona, USA.

Sudbury Herald Messenger. 'Freighter Crew Rescued by Dragon'. CVII: 43:12. Sudbury, Ontario, Canada.

Troutt, Luciana di Costi. 'Pre-natal Nourishment as a Causive Factor in Adult Length in Dragons'. *Zoological Review: Publications in Zoology* 43:8. Royal Institute for the Natural Sciences, Oxford, England.

———. 'Observation Site A3'. *Princeton University Review*. Vol. 3, No. 42. Princeton University, Princeton, New Jersey, USA.

———. 'Verminological Length'. *American Zoological Anatomy* 5:12. Philips Webster Institute, New York, New York, USA.

———. 'Verminological Weight' *American Zoological Anatomy* 6:18. Philips Webster Institute, New York, New York, USA.

United States. Department of Defense Air Force *Bulletin* LCVII:97. US Government Printing Office, Washington, DC, USA.

————. 'Dragon as Target'. *Report* AF736:491:4. US Government Printing Office, Washington, DC, USA.

————. 'Nocturnal Sonic Disturbance, Airborne, Chicopee', Air Defense Command *Bulletin* 7356jk/se998:5. Government Printing Office, Washington, DC, USA.

Yamaguchi Fumio, *Kokuhō no Hogo* (Protecting our National Treasures). Chikuma Shobō, Tōkyō, Japan.

Index